# Family Business as Paradox



Alison-
So fortunate to sit
next to one another at
MWI. Look forward to
connecting & helping
each other!
All the Best-

*We appreciate our families, colleagues and clients for tolerating our temptation to see every problem as a paradox.*

# Family Business as Paradox

Amy Schuman
Stacy Stutz
and
John L. Ward

palgrave
macmillan

First published 2010 by
PALGRAVE MACMILLAN

Palgrave Macmillan in the UK is an imprint of Macmillan Publishers Limited, registered in England, company number 785998, of Houndmills, Basingstoke, Hampshire RG21 6XS.

Palgrave Macmillan in the US is a division of St Martin's Press LLC, 175 Fifth Avenue, New York, NY 10010.

Palgrave Macmillan is the global academic imprint of the above companies and has companies and representatives throughout the world.

Palgrave® and Macmillan® are registered trademarks in the United States, the United Kingdom, Europe and other countries.

ISBN 978-1-349-31853-7 ISBN 978-0-230-29176-8 (eBook)
DOI 10.1057/9780230291768

This book is printed on paper suitable for recycling and made from fully managed and sustained forest sources. Logging, pulping and manufacturing processes are expected to conform to the environmental regulations of the country of origin.

A catalogue record for this book is available from the British Library.

A catalog record for this book is available from the Library of Congress.

10 9 8 7 6 5 4 3 2 1
19 18 17 16 15 14 13 12 11 10

# Contents

*List of figures* *viii*

*List of tables* *x*

*Preface* *xi*

**Introduction – Appreciating Both** **1**

PARADOX CAPACITY AND CAPABILITY 2
PROBLEMS ARE NOT ALL THE SAME 3
PROSPERING IN THE FACE OF AMBIGUITY 7
CAPTURE THE INHERENT TENSION 10
WHAT LIES AHEAD 12

**PART I**

**Acknowledging Both** **15**

WHERE IS YOUR FAMILY BUSINESS' CURRENT FOCUS – FAMILY OR BUSINESS? 17

**1 Which to Choose: Family or Business?** **21**

TO CHOOSE OR NOT TO CHOOSE 22
CHOOSE BOTH 23
FAMILY AND BUSINESS INTERSECTION 26
PARADOX OF INDIVIDUAL *AND* COLLECTIVE 30
INDIVIDUAL *AND* COLLECTIVE IN ACTION 31
CELEBRATING PARADOX AT BERETTA 32
ASSESSMENT SUMMARY 34

**2 Tradition *and* Change in Family Firms** 36

THE GODREJ GROUP: MODEL OF TRADITION *AND* CHANGE 37
DISTINCTIVE TIME ORIENTATION 38
COMPLEX SUCCESSOR DILEMMAS 40
INTERNALLY DRIVEN STRATEGY 42

ENDURING VALUES 44
TRADITION *AND* CHANGE AT BERETTA

**PART II**
**Identifying Both** 49

**3 Predictable Paradoxes Across the Generations** 53

GENERATIONAL OSCILLATION 54
PREDICTABLE PARADOXES: FOUNDER STAGE 56
PREDICTABLE PARADOXES: SIBLING PARTNERSHIP STAGE 61
PREDICTABLE PARADOXES: COUSIN COLLABORATION STAGE 67
THE ENTERPRISING FAMILY 72
GENERATIONAL PARADOXES: FINAL ANALYSIS 74

**4 Predictable Conflicts in the Intersections** 76

FROM TWO SYSTEMS TO THREE 76
PROBLEM–CONFLICT–CONTRADICTION–PARADOX 78
UNDERSTANDING THE INTERSECTIONS 78
FAMILY–MANAGEMENT CONFLICTS 80
MANAGEMENT–OWNERSHIP CONFLICTS 83
OWNERSHIP–FAMILY CONFLICTS 85
GOVERNANCE STRUCTURES 88
INTERSECTIONS: FINAL ANALYSIS 90

**PART III**
**Managing Both** 93

**5 A Continuum for Addressing Paradoxes** 97

EITHER/OR – BOTH/*AND* 98
THE PARADOX MANAGEMENT CONTINUUM 98
FAMILY EMPLOYMENT ON THE CONTINUUM 101
THE ART OF PARADOX MANAGEMENT 107
CYCLE OF RENEWAL AND BENEFIT 114

**6 One Key Tool: The Polarity Map™** 115

ANNA'S FAMILY BUSINESS AND POLARITY MAPPING 115
THE CONTINUUM AND THE MAP 128
ANOTHER POLARITY MAP™: FAMILY COUNCILS 130
STEP BY STEP THROUGH THE POLARITY MAP™ 132
FINAL REFLECTIONS 133

**PART IV**
**Achieving Both** **135**

**7 Experience the Power of Paradox** **139**

SOURCES OF CONTINUITY 139
CULTURE UNLOCKS THE POWER OF PARADOX 141
FROM IMPLICIT TO EXPLICIT 149
A LOOK TOWARD FUSION 150

**Appendices** **153**

APPENDIX A: HISTORICAL PERSPECTIVE ON PARADOX 155
APPENDIX B: PARADOXES IN BUSINESS LITERATURE 167
APPENDIX C: FAMILY FIRST–BUSINESS FIRST ASSESSMENT 185
APPENDIX D: MORE ON POLARITY MAPS™ 193

*Notes* *201*

*Index* *205*

# List of Figures


| | | |
|---|---|---|
| I.1 | Problems and paradoxes | 6 |
| I.2 | Toyota's contradictions | 11 |
| 1.1 | Enterprising family | 25 |
| 1.2 | Family and business: fundamental differences | 26 |
| 1.3 | Examples of family and business conflicts | 28 |
| 1.4 | Common paradoxes in family business | 29 |
| 1.5 | Individual *and* collective paradox | 31 |
| 1.6 | Beretta's paradoxes in action | 33 |
| 2.1 | Time orientation of top management in family firms compared with public firms | 39 |
| 2.2 | Successors' statements of tradition *and* change | 41 |
| 2.3 | Traditional strategy compared with family business strategy formulation | 43 |
| 2.4 | Values comparison | 44 |
| 2.5 | Beretta cultural components | 48 |
| 3.1 | Oscillation in family business focus across generations | 54 |
| 3.2 | Founder Stage fundamental paradoxes | 60 |
| 3.3 | Sibling Partnership Stage fundamental paradoxes | 66 |
| 3.4 | Sample family tree | 67 |
| 3.5 | Cousin Collaboration Stage fundamental paradoxes | 72 |
| 3.6 | Generational oscillation and the Enterprising Family | 73 |
| 3.7 | Summary generational paradoxes | 74 |
| 4.1 | Family business system evolution | 77 |
| 4.2 | Problem–conflict–contradiction–paradox process defined | 78 |
| 4.3 | Intersections in the three subsystems | 79 |
| 4.4 | Family–management conflicts | 80 |
| 4.5 | Management–ownership conflicts | 83 |

4.6 Ownership–family conflicts 86
4.7 Governance structures needed 88

5.1 Paradox management continuum 98
5.2 Family employment 108
5.3 Dividend or distribution policy 110
5.4 Family meetings 112
5.5 Paradox management cycle of renewal 114

6.1 Family internship example: name the poles (sides) 118
6.2 Family internship example: list upsides 119
6.3 Family internship example: list downsides 120
6.4 Family internship: complete Polarity Map™ 124
6.5 Paradox management continuum 129
6.6 Family council composition Polarity Map™ 131

7.1 Classic family business paradoxes 151

B-1 Paradoxes in many of the visionary companies noted in *Built to Last* 177

C-1 Business First–Family First compiled assessment results 191

D-1 Polarity Map™ sequence for handling resistance to change 194
D-2 Polarity Map™ sequence for handling a painful situation 195
D-3 Polarity Map™ sequence for bringing a group together 197
D-4 Blank Polarity Map™ 199

# List of Tables


I.1 Family First–Business First Assessment, Part A: Business Issues for Family Businesses 18
I.1 Family First–Business First Assessment, Part B: Family Issues for Business-Owning Families 19

2.1 Beretta: management of tradition *and* change 46

4.1 Two examples of family–management conflict 81
4.2 Example problems to be solved – family employment 82
4.3 Two examples of management–ownership conflict 84
4.4 Example problems to be solved – board make-up 85
4.5 Two examples of ownership–family conflict 86
4.6 Example problems to be solved –stock ownership 87
4.7 Governance vehicles by intersection 89
4.8 Family business system intersections summary 91

5.1 Paradox management continuum defined 100
5.2 Family employment: application of paradox management 109
5.3 Dividend/distribution policy: application of paradox management 111
5.4 Family meeting: application of paradox management 113

6.1 Step by step through the Polarity Map™ 132

7.1 Sample cultural attributes comparison 144
7.2 Paradoxes and synthesis statements 152

C-1A Family First–Business First Assessment, Part A: Business Issues for Family Businesses 188
C-1B Family First–Business First Assessment, Part B: Family Issues for Business-Owning Families 189
C-2 Business First–Family First Assessment scoring 190

# Preface

*Family Business as Paradox*, this book, is really about **both**. It honors and seeks to achieve what is good for the family, and honors and seeks to achieve what is good for the business. The scale on the cover depicts balancing both the family and the business. This book goes even further, showing how to maximize the positives for both the family and the business. This might seem an unusual approach, because many family businesses feel – or are told – they must choose between business and family in their decision making. That's not to say that choices don't have to be made; making choices is part of any organization. This book's goal is to show that many problems in family businesses are really paradoxes and, in the case of a paradox, it's best to choose **both** sides the paradox comprises, rather than one or the other.

Why is this especially important now? Because family businesses – indeed, all businesses – must be ever more efficient and effective to compete in today's fast-changing global economy. Compromises in fundamental focus compromise success and survival. In addition, more family businesses are reaching later generations and welcoming more family members into management and ownership. These multiple layers of challenge and complexity require more sophisticated governance systems, more thorough succession plans, and more creative methods of financing growth.

How can all this be accomplished? What family businesses need is not a brand-new, simplistic answer, but a return to more classic, time-tested methods of problem solving. Specifically, family businesses are, by nature, replete with problems that are really paradoxes. Learning to identify and to manage paradoxes brings special value to business-owning families and their family businesses. Managing paradoxes requires patience and novel thinking, not prescriptions. And developing the ability to manage paradoxes is crucial for business families who don't want to and need not choose between their business and their family.

A **paradox** is comprised of two sides that *appear to be* opposing, but in fact are mutually supportive.

This book will show that paradoxes are a special kind of problem – and they emerge from naturally occurring conflicts and contradictions in family enterprises. Developing the ability to manage paradoxes requires two types of problem-solving skills. For much of the twentieth century the focus of business was on *algorithmic* problem-solving: rationally defining a problem, identifying its alternatives and selecting the best one. But when we confront a paradox – as is so often the case for family businesses – *heuristic* problem-solving, which uses more experimentation and unique insights, is also necessary.[1] Choosing between algorithmic and heuristic approaches to problem solving is itself an example of paradox. Both approaches are valid and valuable. This book will focus on family business problems that are paradoxes and where heuristic thought processes bring extra insight and benefit. To do this, the book will provide many examples of the paradoxical problems that family businesses face. It will also detail methods to identify and to manage these paradoxes, approaches that should lead to better long-term results for both the family and the business. This will be done in the context of the classic paradoxes family businesses face: growth *versus* liquidity, individual freedom *versus* loyalty to the group, tradition *versus* change, and others. The book will examine these choices in depth, proposing that the superior, long-term answer is both; thus "*versus*" must be replaced by "*and*."

Family businesses are uniquely positioned to harness the energy inherent to paradoxes. That's because family and business are in and of themselves a paradox. The interests of both the family and the business may frequently seem to conflict. Those from business families have known of these conflicts from day one, and thus have built a higher tolerance for the ambiguity contained within business and family conflicts.

Managing paradoxes requires special capacities and capabilities, including a special empathy to see "both sides." For managing paradoxes is as much art as it is science. Thus the book closes by discussing some of the cultural components that will maximize the family business' capacity and capability to manage paradoxes successfully. When family businesses approach very challenging paradoxical problems with curiosity, long-term perspective, world-class problem solving, trust, and extensive communication, they will achieve better solutions – and, more than likely, unique and compelling ones. The family's *capacity* to seek superior, long-term results will strengthen the *bonds* of the family: working together creatively and with mutual respect to find new insights and possibilities brings confidence and pride to the family. And the owning family's *capability* to achieve better results will strengthen the business, propelling it to better performance.

While the models and tools offered in this book are powerful, they are not intended as easy answers. Indeed, many paradoxes lurk amidst the family business world, posing as easily solvable problems, promoting the temptation to manage them away quickly and decisively. But by definition, problems that are paradoxes have no easy solutions. A paradox is comprised of two seemingly opposable truths by nature – thus, picking one alternative over another only allows the underlying issues to fester and, over time, resurface. Suppressing one truth for another only intensifies the tensions between groups of individuals preferring one alternative to the other. For families in business, this greater conflict is rarely acceptable. Thus, learning to successfully accept and manage paradoxes is invaluable.

Paradoxes are typically quite frustrating. Indeed, for a given paradox a family may find no comforting insight and/or reconciliation. In many cases, the paradox must live on, its tensions accepted. That's part of the capacity to live in a world full of paradoxes, capacity which, when coupled with a strong set of family values, pride in the family's traditions and a long-term view, can fuel family business performance and long-term success.

Not surprisingly, paradoxes tend to be found at key points of conflict within a family business. The conflicts families in business face are a natural result of the differences in the interests of three intersecting constituencies: family, management, and ownership. Yet, conflicts at these intersections are often viewed as personal in nature, rather than structural or situational. Natural conflicts also arise as one generation transitions to the next.

These conflicts are inherent; they are predictable, pervasive, and persistent, presenting themselves at some point in the history of every family business. Examples of the problems family businesses face, which we will explore in greater detail, include:

- ❏ Which family members can be employed in the family business?
- ❏ Who will serve on the board?
- ❏ Who will own stock?

If you are a family business member, none of these conflicts are news to you. So what do you do about them? You must learn to manage them. How? Answering that question is the intent of this book – it will walk through key steps in paradox management including, first, identifying the contradictions that are present in family business conflicts and problems to understand the nature of the inherent paradox, and second, using established frameworks and tools to maximize both sides of the paradox. Mastering these steps will help your family business capture the energy in the paradox to both bond your family and propel your business to a successful future.

Amy M. Schuman
Stacy H. Stutz
John L. Ward

# Introduction: Appreciating Both

Although business owners commonly see paradoxes as obstacles to progress, creative problem solvers and scientists see paradoxes differently:

> How wonderful that we have met with a paradox, now we have some hope for making progress.[1]
>
> Niels Bohr

Consider the following common family business problem. The family managers want to retain as much capital in the business as possible, to have reserves against competition and to fund good growth. The family shareholders not working in the business feel the majority of their net worth and personal security are tied up in the business, and thus favor higher dividends. Think of this as the growth and liquidity paradox – seemingly contradicting needs, both valid.

Perhaps a compromise is possible, permitting a limited number of owners to redeem some of their shares back to the company. Neither side is fully satisfied. The business must give up capital, even if only in the short run. Some family members must sell some of their family heirlooms.

Families who manage paradoxes well know that when facing a paradox such as growth *and* liquidity, there is no simple solution, only ongoing management of the tension between the two desirable (and seemingly opposing) options. They know that choosing one side to the exclusion of the other will not make the issue go away permanently. Finding a way to pursue both, although difficult, is the best path forward.

Business-owning families are very familiar with such problems, such contradictions. Managing both family and business seems a constant challenge. So much so, that the term "family business" may be considered an oxymoron, a contradiction within itself: for the family is not usually thought of as a business, and business doesn't represent the full reality of the family.

Despite whatever contradictions the concept of family business may represent, time and time again family businesses achieve extraordinary outcomes. Twenty percent of family businesses continue past the 50-year point,[2] compared with the 15 percent of the S&P 500 that survives to the 40-year mark.[3] Much research concludes that family businesses not only last longer, but drive greater profits than their non-family counterparts.[4] Given all the contradictions they face and the resultant tensions, how can they achieve this?

## PARADOX CAPACITY AND CAPABILITY

Family businesses are successful for many reasons. They have a longer time horizon than most non-family firms, as they view the business as crucial to perpetuating the family into future generations. They have greater consistency in leadership, as the baton is handed from one generation to the next. And they have a strong, supportive culture rooted in the family's traditions and values.[5] These and other factors are some of the reasons why family businesses are so successful, but recognizing these factors doesn't describe *how* the success is achieved.

One of the fundamental reasons family businesses achieve long-term success involves their ability to confront and manage contradictions. Within these contradictions are paradoxes – like the one introduced previously, growth *and* liquidity. Families address these by developing an internal capacity and capability to live and prosper in the face of contradictions and paradoxes – whether they realize it or not.

- ❑ **Capacity** to identify paradoxes and to understand and accept the ambiguity associated with them.
- ❑ **Capability** to use both sides of the paradox to generate greater insights and superior long-term results.

How do family businesses develop this capacity and capability? From our work with family businesses over many decades, across national and cultural boundaries, a theme has emerged: from their inception, family businesses are confronted regularly with paradoxes; the successful ones learn how to manage them effectively.

Why does this phenomenon surface in family businesses in particular? Because, although the family and the business need each other to achieve long-term success and fulfillment, they represent inherently divergent points of view. When family businesses are confronted with problems, two perspectives typically emerge that appear to be in conflict – that of the family and that of the business. Upon closer consideration, however, these two viewpoints prove to be not mutually exclusive but mutually supportive. Thus, a family business, a family and its business, is the "ultimate paradox." This book will explore, in depth, the common paradoxes that confront family businesses. It also will provide a variety of approaches that family businesses can use to develop the capacity and capability to manage these paradoxes.

The capacity and capability to manage paradoxes relies on four foundational factors:

- First, there must be recognition that not all problems should be treated the same way – some are clear problems to solve, others are paradoxes to manage.
- Second, there must be appreciation and acceptance of the ambiguity and uncertainty inherent to paradox – the rush to resolve the situation must be resisted.
- Third, there must be acceptance – even appreciation – of the inherent tension in the two seemingly opposing sides of the paradox; this tension contains useful energy that can be harnessed to bond the family and propel the business to long-term success.
- Finally, people must develop the necessary skills and abilities to manage the paradoxes successfully.

## PROBLEMS ARE NOT ALL THE SAME

In many walks of life, and particularly in business, people have been trained in techniques and tools intended to *solve* problems. Be clear, be decisive, be firm, and make the tough call! The reality is that once it appears a given problem has been solved, a new problem often surfaces that drives the situation back to its original state, or some close approximation. Think of how often organizations alternate between centralized and decentralized models, or between outsourcing and insourcing, just to name two examples. In family businesses, how often do family members working in the business have "discussions" about how things need to change versus keeping the status quo? If there is agreement about making desired changes, how often do these changes stick? This is a classic struggle or tension between tradition *and* change – a key family business paradox discussed in detail in Chapter 2.

Such changes in organization or sourcing or tradition-based approaches are responses to a specific problem – perhaps to improve efficiency, customer focus, or quality control. But when a new or related problem develops (as it inevitably will), the pendulum begins to swing back in the opposite direction. As the saying goes, "If you don't like this month's organization, just wait for next month's" – or the adage of "top management's flavor of the month."

This book looks at a specific type of problem, one encountered constantly by family businesses: a paradox, or a problem with two perceived contradictory truths. The word "paradox" is derived from the Greek "para," meaning "beyond," and "doxa," meaning "idea." Thus a paradox contains two things that when considered together defy what one would think is possible; the paradox goes beyond conventional ideas. Although the two truths that comprise a given paradox appear to be contradictory, upon further analysis the contradictions are found not to be contradictory at all, but mutually supportive. For this book's purposes, the definition of paradox is as follows:

> A **paradox** is comprised of two sides that *appear to be* opposing, but in fact are mutually supportive.

Consider the following examples. In family life, a common contradiction is that of roots *and* wings: parents are eager for their children to have strong connections to their home and family; yet they also know the importance of encouraging independence and experimentation. How can both be achieved? Another familiar contradiction, presented at the opening of this Introduction, is growth *and* liquidity. How can this paradox be addressed successfully?

A familiar business paradox is short term *and* long term. In their book *The Three Tensions*, Dodd and Favaro identify this as one of three key tensions or paradoxes that all businesses need to address.[6] Peter Drucker illustrates this paradox well, in noting that a good manager:

> must, so to speak, keep his nose to the grindstone while lifting his eyes to the hills – which is quite an acrobatic feat.[7]

Although such contortions seem almost impossible, they are, in fact, frequently required.

Generally, the first step in developing the capacity to manage a paradox is gaining a deeper awareness and understanding of how paradoxes work. Paradoxes are a particular kind of problem comprised of two interdependent truths. The two sides of a paradox appear to be in conflict because of the tension between them. However, on closer examination, the two apparently conflicting sides of a paradox are found to be mutually supportive.

Since both sides of a paradox are needed, choosing one to the exclusion of the other is not an ideal approach. In fact, choosing only one side of a paradox gives rise to more problems. The tension between the two sides of a paradox cannot be eliminated – a paradox can't be "solved," but it can (and must) be actively managed. In fact, paradoxes must be managed on an ongoing basis, as they have no specific endpoint.

Dr. Barry Johnson[8] was one of the first practitioners to recognize and write about this distinction. His exploration of "problems without solutions" was groundbreaking for both individuals and organizations across the globe. As Dr. Johnson points out, most problems, once solved, do not require ongoing consideration, nor must they be "re-solved" on a regular basis. They are comprised of two or more alternatives that are not dependent, and thus these types of problems are solvable, with endpoints. Figure I.1 (overleaf) distinguishes solvable problems from paradoxes, which require a distinct approach.

Greg Page, the CEO of Cargill, understands that paradoxes must be managed, not solved, and the potential benefit to the business of approaching problems in this way. Mr. Page introduced these concepts to his management team and the Cargill organization worldwide. Cargill

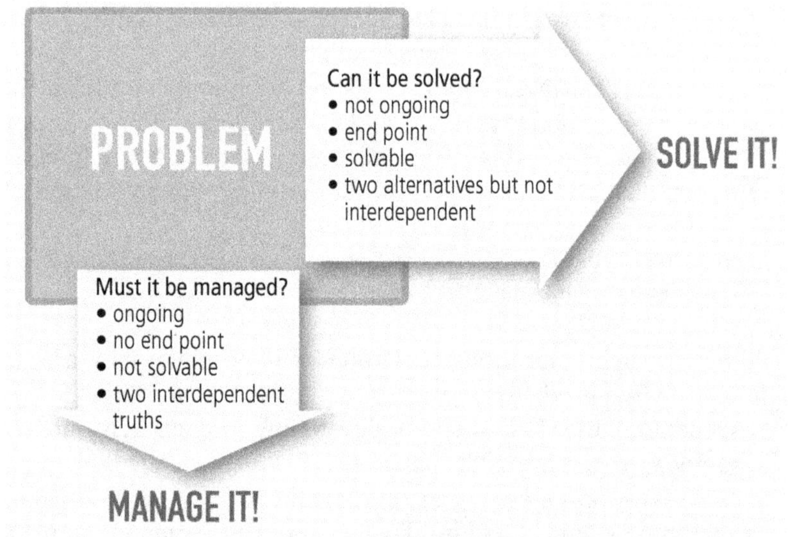


**Figure I.1** *Problems and paradoxes*
*Source:* Based on Dr. Barry Johnson and Polarity Management Associates.[8]

was established in 1865; with US$116.6 billion in global revenues in 2009, it is the largest privately held family-founded company in the world. Page's commitment to understanding and handling paradoxes differently is described in the following excerpt from a *Cargill News* article written by Mr. Page to the Cargill employees.

> We all like certainty. We enjoy identifying a problem, solving it and moving on to the next problem. Thankfully, this problem-solving skill is a real strength at Cargill.
>
> The world, however, doesn't always cooperate. More than 2000 years ago, observers like Plato realized that the world involves paradoxes. Authors like Fitzgerald gave eloquence to the insight, and more recently, business leaders are recognizing paradoxes are a necessary part of our corporate lives.
>
> "The test of a first-rate intelligence is the ability to hold two opposing ideas in the mind at the same time and still retain the ability to function."
> F. Scott Fitzgerald
>
> A paradox involves two interdependent opposites. Both points of view are

> accurate, but neither is complete. In fact, both points of view are essential for either of them to be successful.
>
> A simple example is cost vs. quality. A single-minded focus on either extreme is going to result in unhappy customers or business ruin. We must both seek the optimum quality and still make our products affordable. This fluid situation changes as circumstances change. There is no one finally "right" answer.
>
> This is not just a philosophic musing; rather this is how companies must operate to be successful.
>
> I started this discussion about paradoxes four years ago at Cargill's global management meeting. I had been getting many pleas for certainty, and I could see the energy people were wasting in a search for finality. It is wasteful, and even wrong, for Cargill to act, as one business unit leader wonderfully expressed it "with a false sense of concreteness."
>
> In this world full of paradoxes, companies that manage paradoxes well out-perform companies that don't. But we can't manage paradoxes until we identify the difference between a paradox and a problem.[9]

As Mr. Page points out, it's important to understand the difference between ordinary problems and paradoxes, and to distinguish between the two. In a world of problems, one must discriminate between those that can and should be solved and those which must be addressed differently because they represent a specific type of problem – a paradox. Following this logic, not all problems encountered *are* paradoxes. However, those that are paradoxes require a different approach, one that does not focus on any single choice or solution.

The traditional approach to problem-solving, decision-making, and choosing solutions, used alone, is not effective in the case of a paradox. As psychiatrist and author Erich Fromm suggested, "the quest for certainty blocks the search for meaning. Uncertainty is the very condition to impel man to unfold his powers."[10] Recognizing paradoxes for what they are reveals the energy they contain. Harnessing that energy will strengthen the bonds of the family and propel the business to better performance.

## PROSPERING IN THE FACE OF AMBIGUITY

The capacity to manage paradoxes requires an appreciation and acceptance of the ambiguity paradoxes contain. The rush to resolve the paradox must be resisted. This can be difficult for family business members. Rarely are ambiguous problems or those open to more than one interpretation welcomed in the business world. Most successful businesses have spent years developing laser-sharp approaches that can yield rapid and efficient problem solving. Their processes seek to identify the source of a problem, generate recommendations in response, then identify and implement the optimal decision – often involving a "tough call."

With ambiguity comes uncertainty, and with uncertainty there is often a need to make assumptions. Making assumptions in an effort to eliminate the uncertainty that accompanies a paradox will likely cause additional problems. A focus on eliminating uncertainty is especially prominent early in life and career, as most ideas and opinions are based on formulas and rational problem-solving processes learned in the classroom and in books. In the case of a problem that is not clear, the common approach is to create a list of pros and cons, count up the number in each column, and choose the option with the most pros or the least cons. This is an example of an algorithmic approach to problem solving.

If only it were that simple in the case of paradoxical problems. In choosing the option with the greatest number of pros, consider what happens to the cons associated with that choice, or the pros of the opposite side, especially if it is a paradox. Abandoning one side of a paradox in favor of a "solution" is what ultimately causes another problem to surface in time. Why does this happen?

It happens because making a choice that seemingly clears things up (that is, by eliminating any ambiguity) is what is expected of strong business leaders; it's a key criterion organizations use to reward those in charge. But in reality, making a choice when dealing with a paradox will likely kick off a new phase of the problem's lifecycle. In "clearing things up" by choosing one side of the paradox, the decision maker inadvertently grants power to the opposite side of the paradox. In fact, the non-chosen side of the paradox will continue to gain power over time, until it emerges as a new problem – or a new phase of the old problem. It happens because business professionals are taught to "make things clear," rather than being willing to live with ambiguity and harness the power it may contain.

"Scenarios: uncharted waters ahead," a two-part *Harvard Business Review* article, highlights Royal Dutch Shell's sophisticated scenario forecasting technique as critical to the company's success. The article points out that it wasn't an algorithmic method alone that was the source of the success:

> The way to solve this problem was not to … [perfect] techniques …. Too many forces work against getting the right forecast. The future is no longer stable; it has become a moving target. No single right [answer] can be deduced from past behavior … the better approach … is to accept uncertainty, try to understand it, and make it part of our reasoning. Uncertainty today is not just an occasional, temporary deviation from a reasonable predictability; it is a basic "structure" feature of the business environment …. [The key is to] structure uncertainty [and] change the decision makers' assumptions about the way the world works and compel them to [reorient] their mental model of reality …. [Such a] willingness to face uncertainty and to understand the forces driving it requires an almost revolutionary transformation in a large organization.[11]

The company drove success through a combination of the managers' methods and approach – they integrated algorithmic work (the method) with heuristic work (the approach). This illustrates the idea presented earlier that for paradoxes, it is necessary to use both algorithmic method *and* heuristic approach.

Shell clearly understood the imperative to live with the ambiguity that is part of many situations, and to identify and accept it as part of the reality of the situation. In the context of paradox, we should resist the pull toward finding a "solution," and make the ambiguity and tension present work for the organization or the family. As suggested earlier, this goes against how most business professionals are trained in school or on the job. Managers are expected to "answer the question," or "perform a task," or "make a clear choice or decision," not to find a way to live with more questions than answers.

It's worth emphasizing that not all problems are meant to be solved, in the traditional sense. The idea of uncovering all the facts for the purposes of reducing or eliminating uncertainty, in order to begin to solve a problem, is not realistic in cases of paradox. Rather, it's important to recognize the ambiguity or uncertainty experienced as a clue to the presence of a paradox. Then, rather than seeking an answer to restore a sense of comfort, embrace the ambiguity. How can this be accomplished?

Back to the *Cargill News* article cited earlier, to an excerpt in which Mr. Page acknowledges what happens in the face of ambiguity and provides some advice for handling it:

> Paradoxes can be frustrating – no doubt about it – but we ignore them at our peril. We must face them, aggressively manage them to capture the positives they offer, and learn to perform in the ambiguity they bring.
>
> The way to deal with the ambiguity is not by demanding clarity, but through active communication – - trusting each other to speak openly and listen responsibly to determine if an issue is a problem or a paradox.[12]

When dealing with a paradox, it is a given that there will be uncertainty. Don't push it aside; rather, accept the ambiguity, then seek out the tensions imbedded within the paradox.

## CAPTURE THE INHERENT TENSION

Family firms with a well-developed capability for managing paradoxes are very adept at accepting – even appreciating – the tension contained in the two seemingly opposing sides of the paradox. They understand that this tension contains useful energy that can be harnessed to bond the family and propel the business.

No two things are as closely related as opposites: hot and cold, love and hate, war and peace. The study of contradiction over the centuries has cut across many areas of thinking, including philosophy, science, and mathematics. For further information and insights regarding historical paradoxes, see Appendix A, "Historical Perspective on Paradox."

Georg Wilhelm Friedrich Hegel, the nineteenth-century German philosopher, asserted a then-controversial approach to philosophy and history, a perspective still highly relevant today. In Hegel's view,

> Change was the rule of life. Every idea, every force, irrepressibly bred its opposite, and the two merged into a "unity" that in turn produced its own contradiction. And history was nothing but the expression of this flux of conflicting and resolving ideas and forces.[13]

Whether or not we agree with Hegel's view of history as a naturally dialectical process, his central insight is useful in managing paradoxes.

Inherent to paradox is contradiction, which begs the question of whether two seemingly opposing forces, when addressed together, can be integrated, synthesized, and in some cases even fused for the long run. Before answering that question, it's important to understand its implication: that in the long run, contradictions can be integrated, or in some cases fused. Underlying this notion is the idea that over an infinite – or at least very long – time horizon (as typically embraced by family businesses), contradictions no longer seem to exist, as their opposing sides can meld together.

In the short run, however, real tension points are experienced as contradictory forces push and pull from both sides of the paradox. As mentioned earlier, the key is to recognize this tension and use it as an advantage, keeping in mind that over time, this tension, or these opposite forces, have the potential of resolving themselves and even of becoming mutually supportive. This is the potential power of the contradictions within a paradox.

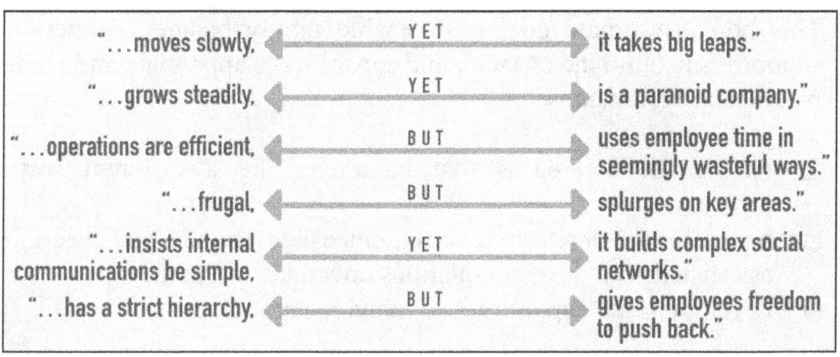


**Figure I.2** *Toyota's contradictions*

A recent *Harvard Business Review* article presents a compelling example of how actively managing contradictions can lead to superior results. The article, "The contradictions that drive Toyota's success," describes a company culture that is at once "stable and paranoid, systematic and experimental, formal and frank," and concludes that Toyota's historical success is in large part due to "its ability to embrace contradictions like these."[14] In other words, Toyota uses the tensions created by opposing ideas, or contradictions, to generate new and innovative ways to deal with the issues it faces.[15] Figure I.2 highlights several of the contradictions noted, in the form of paradox, that fuel Toyota's innovation.

The article confirms that "Toyota deliberately fosters contradictory viewpoints … and challenges employees to find solutions by transcending differences rather than resorting to compromises." This approach is a radical departure from how most businesses are run. Moreover, this transcending of differences is the key to fusing a paradox, or melding its seemingly opposite sides. The article goes further to suggest that "companies have no choice but to embrace contradictions as a way of life," and "develop routines to resolve contradictions." These conclusions are true for all businesses. But they are especially true for family businesses, as family firms have lived the fundamental paradox of family *and* business daily, since the business began.

## WHAT LIES AHEAD

This book's ultimate goal is to enable family business leaders and supporters to build the capacity and capability to appreciate and manage paradoxes. That means:

- having the awareness that paradoxes are a different sort of problem.
- being able to tolerate and even embrace the ambiguity and uncertainty associated with the contradictions imbedded in a paradox.
- developing the capabilities to manage paradoxes.

This is reflected in the book's more specific objectives and structure, as outlined below.

- To help readers understand that interest in paradoxes is not new. Paradoxes have been studied through most of history and discussed in depth in modern business contexts. They are recognized as key factors in success, especially in times of great change. (Appendices A and B)
- To recognize that family business is a paradox in and of itself, and that family firms are filled with paradoxes that must be managed actively, rather than solved. (Chapter 1)

- To take an in-depth look at one paradox that poses particular challenges – and opportunities – for family businesses: the paradox of tradition *and* change is found in all organizations, but has special significance for family enterprises. (Chapter 2)
- To identify the special challenges family businesses face in the form of paradoxes, by listing a set of classic conflicts and paradoxes that are predictable, pervasive and persistent. These challenges emerge from:
  - The generational evolution of the business (Chapter 3)
  - The interaction of the three main subsystems in family businesses – family, management and ownership. (Chapter 4)
- To introduce methods and tools to manage the continuum of paradox options from Either/Or to Both/*AND* ends of the spectrum. (Chapters 5 and 6)
- To explore some of the components of family and business cultures that are most conducive to the management of paradoxes. (Chapter 7)
- To make the argument that, with curiosity and practice, family businesses can harness the tensions and conflicts from paradox-based contradictions to strengthen family bonds and propel business success. (entire book)

The book is organized into four parts. Part I details *why* family businesses are uniquely positioned to address paradoxes and to reap their benefits. Part II identifies *what* paradoxes will likely be encountered as generations transition and as the family-manager-owner system evolves. Part III shows *how* to manage paradoxes with specific frameworks and tools. Part IV, the Conclusion, considers *when* the culture of a business and of a family is most supportive of successful paradox management.

*This page intentionally left blank*

# Part I

# Acknowledging Both

*This page intentionally left blank*

A self-assessment inventory appears as Table I.1 on pages 18 and 19. It would be most helpful to take the assessment now, to place your current operating approach in greater perspective.

Often, when working with a new concept, the easiest way to make it real and to ensure understanding is to apply it.

> We need a new way of thinking about our problems and our futures. My suggestion is the management of paradox, in that paradox can only be "managed" in the sense of coping with. Manage always did mean "coping with," until we purloined the word to mean "planning and control."
>
> Paradox I now see to be inevitable, endemic and perpetual. The more turbulent the times, the more complex the world, the more paradoxes there are. We can, and should, reduce the starkness of some of the contradictions, minimize the inconsistencies, understand the puzzles in the paradoxes, but we cannot make them disappear, or solve them completely, or escape from them. Paradoxes are like the weather, something to be lived with, not solved, the worst aspects mitigated, the best enjoyed and used as clues to the way forward. Paradox has to be accepted, coped with and made sense of, in life, work and in the community and among nations.
>
> Charles Handy, *The Age of Paradox* (1994)[1]

## WHERE IS YOUR FAMILY BUSINESS'S CURRENT FOCUS – FAMILY OR BUSINESS?

Before beginning, know that there is no "right" answer for any of the questions posed. When considering the question and the associated choices, please mark where on the continuum (from 1 to 5) you believe your family business is *currently* operating. It is important to answer every question. So, if a question leaves you confused or indifferent, please score it a 3. When you have completed all 28 questions, please total your score at the bottom of each page.

The assessment will be revisited at the end of Chapter 1. Note that the results of the inventory can be used to help business families move beyond seeing problems and conflicts as personal in nature and to begin creating systems and structures that reconcile or integrate divergent points of view – as is the case for paradox-based problems.

Appendix C provides instructions on completing and scoring the assessment. It also discusses how to interpret your scores and highlights trends across family businesses, cultures and generations. It also includes observations based on the thousands of times the survey has been administered to students and clients worldwide.

**Table I.1** ***Family First–Business First Assessment, Part A: Business Issues for Family Businesses***

| | | | | | | | |
|---|---|---|---|---|---|---|---|
| 1 | Are you generous with shareholders in providing them with liquidity and dividends? | 1 | 2 | 3 | 4 | 5 | Or do you favor retention of capital in the business? |
| 2 | If a shareholder wants to redeem, does the share valuation formula provide a high price? | 1 | 2 | 3 | 4 | 5 | Or do you seek to keep shares at a low value? |
| 3 | Does your business focus on current profitability? | 1 | 2 | 3 | 4 | 5 | Or more on long-term growth? |
| 4 | Do you prefer a few diverse businesses? | 1 | 2 | 3 | 4 | 5 | Or one focused business? |
| 5 | Is your business mostly domestic? | 1 | 2 | 3 | 4 | 5 | Or are you more global? |
| 6 | Does your business prefer public privacy? | 1 | 2 | 3 | 4 | 5 | Or see visible public relations as important? |
| 7 | Do you prefer the decision-making speed of a private company? | 1 | 2 | 3 | 4 | 5 | Or the discipline and accountability of public ownership? |
| 8 | Do you do business with relatives who are suppliers or vendors or advisors? | 1 | 2 | 3 | 4 | 5 | Or prefer a strict no conflicts of interest policy? |
| 9 | Does your company regard loyalty highly? | 1 | 2 | 3 | 4 | 5 | Or, more so, celebrate achievement and merit? |
| 10 | Do you offer non-family executives a sense of career security? | 1 | 2 | 3 | 4 | 5 | Or reward them with stock options? |
| 11 | Are your decisions based heavily on family values? | 1 | 2 | 3 | 4 | 5 | Or, more so, on maximizing share price value? |
| 12 | Are you more respectful of tradition? | 1 | 2 | 3 | 4 | 5 | Or a promoter of change? |
| 13 | Is wealth preservation a key objective of owners? | 1 | 2 | 3 | 4 | 5 | Or is entrepreneurship more the focus? |
| 14 | Do you look for independent directors who are supportive in nature? | 1 | 2 | 3 | 4 | 5 | Or those who are more dispassionately critical of decisions and policies? |
| | Total score: | | | | | | |

***Source:*** Family First/Business First Assessment, John L. Ward, Family Business Consulting Group, 1999.

**Table I.1** ***Family First–Business First Assessment, Part B: Family Issues for Business-Owning Families***

| | | | | | | | |
|---|---|---|---|---|---|---|---|
| 1 | Do you welcome family employment regardless of work experience or educational qualifications? | 1 | 2 | 3 | 4 | 5 | Or have very selective family employment requirements before joining the business? |
| 2 | Is dissent accepted among family members so that different folks may express different views to management? | 1 | 2 | 3 | 4 | 5 | Or does the family attempt to be of one voice in communications to managers in the business? |
| 3 | Is ownership passed on by family branch (per stirpes)? | 1 | 2 | 3 | 4 | 5 | Or are there efforts that family members of future generations will have more equal ownership (per capita) regardless of size of different branches? |
| 4 | In decision making, is there respect for elders? | 1 | 2 | 3 | 4 | 5 | Or more aggressive "take charge" leadership? |
| 5 | Are non-employed owners involved in business decision making? | 1 | 2 | 3 | 4 | 5 | Or quite "hands off"? |
| 6 | Do family members feel that the business is part of their identity? | 1 | 2 | 3 | 4 | 5 | Or feel very autonomous from the business? |
| 7 | Does the family show a high standard of living? | 1 | 2 | 3 | 4 | 5 | Or deliberately attempt to understate its wealth? |
| 8 | Are policies and rules for family members flexible? | 1 | 2 | 3 | 4 | 5 | Or quite formal and precise? |
| 9 | Is compensation of family members private? | 1 | 2 | 3 | 4 | 5 | Or openly disclosed to family members and to managers? |
| 10 | Are there many unspoken topics and issues among family members? | 1 | 2 | 3 | 4 | 5 | Or open communications? |
| 11 | Is family attendance at family business events voluntary? | 1 | 2 | 3 | 4 | 5 | Or expected or required? |
| 12 | Does the extended family spend lots of time with each other away from the business? | 1 | 2 | 3 | 4 | 5 | Or do folks spend most all of their personal time with their nuclear family? |
| 13 | Do family members see the business as creating opportunities for personal freedom? | 1 | 2 | 3 | 4 | 5 | Or does it give them more a sense of personal responsibility? |
| 14 | Do family members use company resources for personal use? | 1 | 2 | 3 | 4 | 5 | Or is use of expense accounts, employees, or vehicles for personal use prohibited? |
| | Total score: | | | | | | |

***Source:*** Family First/Business First Assessment, John L. Ward, Family Business Consulting Group, 1999.

# 1 Which to Choose: Family or Business?

There's a common question in the world of family business: family first or business first?

> There is yet another spin to this paradox that I have found intriguing – that opposites not only coexist, but can even enhance one another.[1]
>
> Richard Farson, *Management of the Absurd*

How to answer this question? Family business members don't want to decide because they know the likely negative effects on the business and/or the family of choosing one over the other. Similarly, family business consultants who have observed family businesses at various stages of development across the globe know it's actually a trick question, and that the best answer is to choose both – family first *and* business first.

At its core, the science (and art) of running a successful family business is to manage or cope (as suggested by Charles Handy in the quote that opens this Part of the book) with the inherent paradoxes, or perceived contradictory truths, that make family firms so special. What does this really mean?

Much of the answer lies in successfully mixing family and business. This is the fundamental challenge – one best viewed as an opportunity. The family system has a set of norms, beliefs, and values. Business systems typically have a very different set of norms, beliefs, and values. As a result, these two systems behave in distinct ways that can conflict and give rise to many challenges. So, when issues arise between family and business, members often feel forced to choose one or the other. What's more, many family business experts will advise family businesses to choose, with some arguing that the *only* choice is the business. After all, they reason, if the business is harmed, what's left? Current business-related more algorithmic thinking generally supports this view, by providing processes, tools, and techniques that focus on solving problems, mostly by choosing one specific alternative. Other advisors will argue that the only choice is the family: why own a business if it fractures the family?

## TO CHOOSE OR NOT TO CHOOSE

Business professionals, for the most part, have been trained to choose an alternative. They do this by analyzing the positives and negatives of each option, along with the likely outcomes. For argument's sake, that approach can be applied to the question of focus here: family *or* business?

### Choose business

First, consider the advice of experts who recommend that someone facing this dilemma choose business. This may make sense intuitively, as without a successful business there may be nothing to support the family and their ongoing needs. The focus "should be" on the bottom line, because it's the only objective measure that assures fairness to all stakeholders. Yet it is not unusual in these cases (that is, extreme business-first focus) for the business eventually to be sold, likely in the second or third generation.

How does this come to be? First, consider that in later generations only a few family members are likely sufficiently competent for, or interested in, management and governance roles in the business. Perhaps ownership control is concentrated in the hands of the operating managers. Thus the capital may be more likely to be kept in the business for company safety and growth. In a typical scenario, then, the family members not involved in the business begin to feel alienated, or ill-trusted, or even gullible to leave all their wealth at risk. As a result, the business is likely to be sold in the second or third generation, or the disgruntled shareholders are bought out – typically at a valuation that they feel is unfair. In the worst case, a lawsuit ensues. The natural result is a fractured family and a business that's either very distracted or weakened by the need to raise funds for its sale or redemption of shares by departing family members. At best, the company becomes a business only for some of the family.

Does this alternative yield what most family businesses are aiming for? Not likely.

### Choose family

What happens when the other side of the family-business coin is chosen, prioritizing the family's needs over those of the business? Consider a family business whose core business is manufacturing. Assume that the manufacturing plant needs to upgrade its factory technology at the same time that several of the founder's children (who work in the business) have children of their own and require or want higher salaries to support their growing families. There is not enough financial flexibility within the business to make both investments.

In choosing family needs over business needs, through salary increases or higher dividends, this family business would forgo equipment upgrades that could enhance the company's long-term prospects, using the money instead for family security and welfare. Further, there will likely come a time when ill-prepared or unqualified family members will seek top-management positions. The family, having established a precedent of family-first, may not be able to say "no." As a result, more qualified family may look for careers outside of the business and the best non-family executives will likely depart for better or more "fairly" managed opportunities.

Choosing family systematically over the business in the long run will likely cause business performance problems and ultimately family disintegration. The weakened and distracted business is likely to be eventually sold, typically at a deep discount. The end results are the same as those linked to prioritizing business consistently over family. Both approaches miss the mark.

## CHOOSE BOTH

There is a third choice. This choice, based on mutual inclusion and necessity, is to choose both. It can be accomplished by inserting the word "*and*" within the term "family business" – family *and* business. This is referred to as a Both/*AND* approach. How might a Both/

*AND* approach play out in a particular family business? Consider the following situation.

A banking family was developing its business strategy and had to decide on the appropriate number of business locations or outlets. In considering the needs of the community, the business's economics, and the fact that there were five siblings actively engaged in the business, the family chose to have a total of five locations. This approach to strategy formulation is very different from how strategic planning is typically taught in business school.

A typical MBA strategic planning approach would start by assessing the organization's internal capabilities, then move on to understanding the external environmental forces, analyzing the industry and markets, and so on. Yet this family's strategy worked very well: the bank's five locations prospered and the family enjoyed harmonious relationships.

So, was the family's approach wrong? No. On the contrary, it could be considered a highly creative family business response, one that granted each child some level of autonomy while simultaneously serving the community and growing the business. Of course, this approach may not have been the easiest or most streamlined solution. In the short run, the family faced many challenges and a great deal of work to accommodate this new structure. Among the questions they faced: How to pay each other if roles and performance levels weren't equivalent? How to share precious resources – cash and talent – across their portfolio? How to make key decisions at the top, the holding company level? And more. Despite these challenges, over the long run the strategy has yielded significant advantages.

Furthermore, it's likely that, in the end, no one will remember exactly how the number of branches was established, or the complexity and frustrations of making it work. As importantly, there probably is not much conscious awareness of how the process of wrestling with these challenges helped the family increase their capacity to face future tough questions together and, as a result, increased their overall capability to address other tricky contradictions that come with running a business together. However, their determination to honor both the family *and* the business through this approach (whether consciously or not) certainly contributes to their continued success.

This simple example demonstrates the power of embracing both. The family business used a Both/*AND* approach rather than an Either/

Or approach. (More on this in Chapter 5.) They allowed the tensions present in their effort to both bond them more closely together AND propel the business toward the family's longer-term vision – one in which the third generation will be proud of their heritage and their contributions to the welfare of their communities. This type of paradoxical management is core to the successful evolution of a business family into an "Enterprising Family."

An Enterprising Family is one that integrates a family-first *and* business-first orientation. It achieves a unique competitive advantage by building both its capacity and capability to manage paradoxes. Figure 1.1 presents a visual depiction of these ideas.

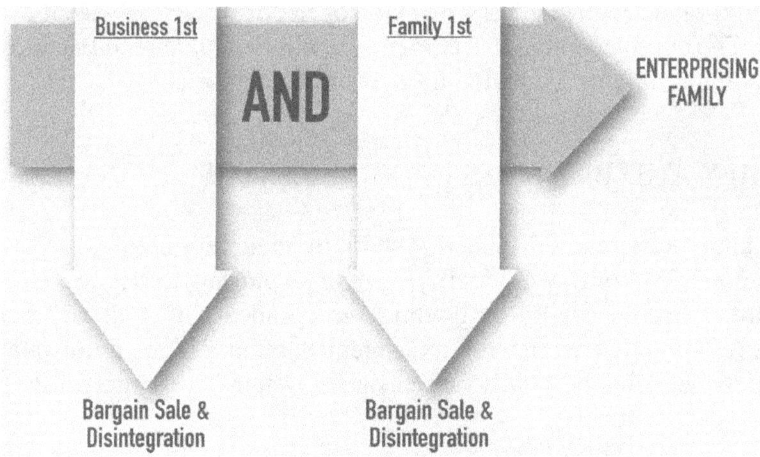


**Figure 1.1** *Enterprising family*

An Enterprising Family includes family-first *and* business-first thinking by creating a portfolio of diverse opportunities that suit the unique talents and interests of family members wishing to participate. With a variety of opportunities, family members who are not interested or skilled in business can still be included in meaningful ways. They can help lead the family's philanthropy efforts or its family council, for example. Thus, those not engaged in the business have roles and make contributions that are also valued. As a result, they conclude that it's best for the family to protect the interests of the business and it's best for the business to engage the family.

Put another way, those not inclined to be involved in the business see the benefits of a business-first point of view for the family. And those involved in leading the business see the benefits of a family-first point of view for the business. Such viewpoints keep the family owners engaged in the family, loyal to the business, and proud of both the business *and* the family.

As should be clear by now, family businesses inherently face many paradoxes. Yet the idea is not just to choose both sides of a given paradox, then sit back and watch as the contradictions magically disappear. A great deal of effort is involved. Sustained and thoughtful effort can, over time, lead to a successful integration or coming together of these seemingly opposite sides. So, when presented with a problem that is a paradox, rather than choosing one side or the other, actively seek both sides. The alternative to not seeking both will be to live with the fallout – ongoing problems generated by the side not chosen.

## FAMILY AND BUSINESS INTERSECTION

The family system and business system, by their very nature, are filled with potential conflicts. Identifying and exploring these provides a helpful backdrop for understanding the paradoxes that family businesses commonly encounter. For a general summary of the fundamental conflicts between the family and business systems, see Figure 1.2.

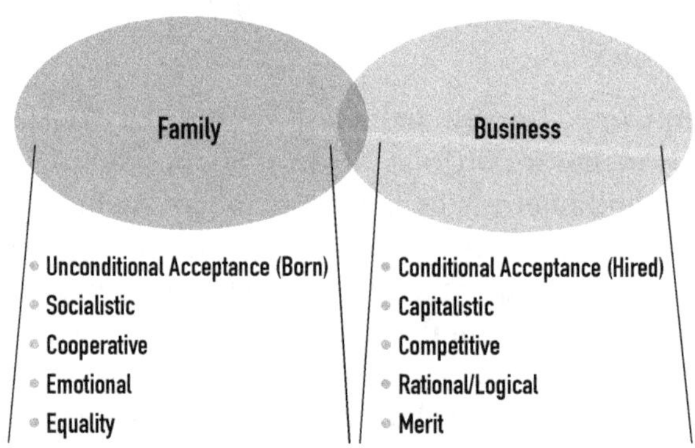


**Figure 1.2** *Family and business: fundamental differences*

As noted in Figure 1.2, one area of conflict is that of acceptance. The family system is based on unconditional acceptance; members are born into the family, and thus accepted as they are. Business systems, in contrast, revolve around conditional acceptance; people are invited (in other words, hired) into the business, and retained, based on specific criteria.

Another conflict, which in many ways sums up the broader set of differences between the two systems, is that families are inherently socialistic and businesses are inherently capitalistic. The world of family business essentially attempts to mix the norms of socialism and capitalism. Built into the differences between these ideologies are several others differences worth mentioning, which often surface as a family business evolves. Families are largely cooperative, while business tends to be competitive. Families operate more from an emotional base, while businesses operate more from a logical base. Most families seek equality of results for family members; businesses make decisions based on merit. (As an aside, addressing the paradox of equality and merit may require focusing on fair opportunities rather than fair results – Chapter 4 offers more about how to approach this paradox.)

When bringing together two systems that have very different, even seemingly opposite, approaches and beliefs, there is bound to be conflict. Family businesses are no exception. As logic and many observations reveal, conflict is innate in this context: most family businesses face multiple conflicts at many points in time. Yet there's comfort in the fact that these conflicts tend to be predictable, even inevitable, and surface at times when thinking about an issue from the family perspective and the business perspective generates two seemingly opposite points of view.

These predictable conflicts within family businesses (as noted in Figure 1.3 overleaf) can be quite damaging if not anticipated and proactively managed. One of the conflicts is leadership succession or generational transition. The family prefers a member of the family's next generation to take over, while the business seeks someone with a specific set of qualifications. What's more, there is often additional conflict related to the actual handover from one leader to another. Sometimes the older regime hangs around for longer than they should, making it difficult for the new leader to gain the full respect and attention of the rest of the management team and organization.

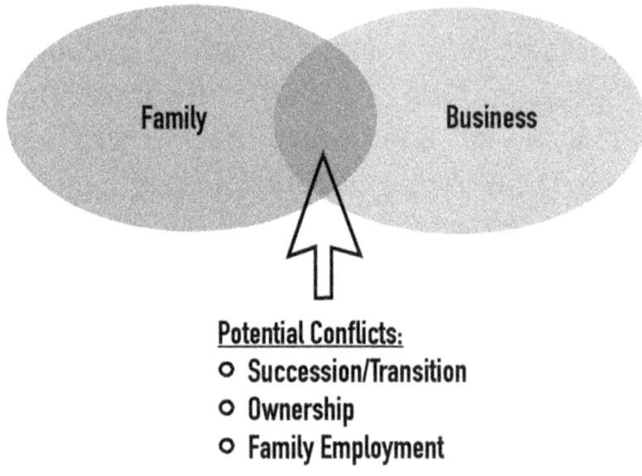


**Figure 1.3** *Examples of family and business conflicts*

Succession and transition can be especially difficult in earlier generations, as the ownership and involvement of the family is quite concentrated and all involved have an intense, vested interest in the outcome.

Another near-universal trigger of conflict in family businesses is the topic of ownership, especially in regards to managing the expectations of the ownership group. There is typically significant tension about who gets how much economic interest in the business and who gets how much voting power. The family may believe that everything should be divided equally across family members. The business perspective may be quite different: ownership should be divided in a way that enables the business to be productive, rewarding those who make the greatest contributions to performance. It may also be that those working in the business have specific beliefs about how ownership interest and power should be concentrated, while those not in the business day-to-day hold another point of view. These seemingly opposite beliefs about ownership can, if left unmanaged, create damaging conflict. This is especially likely in later generations, when the ownership group often becomes quite large and geographically dispersed.

An additional common area of conflict is employment of family members. The family view is that family members should have employment opportunities regardless of circumstances. The business perspective is that employment should be based on the skills and qualifications of the individual and business needs. How should such potential conflicts and contradictions be handled?

These family business conflicts are not just problems, they have the characteristics of a paradox: there is truth to both sides of the contradiction. It's important to look at all factors related to the contradictions, to avoid making a specific choice or decision that one side or the other won't accept. This means avoiding trade-offs as well, where more of this means less of that, and choosing between this or that will result in a suboptimal outcome. So, an optimal approach starts with recognizing these contradiction-rich situations as being comprised of two sides that appear to be in conflict but in fact are mutually supportive paradoxes as shown in Figure 1.4. Taking this approach maximizes the chances of best serving both the family *and* the business.

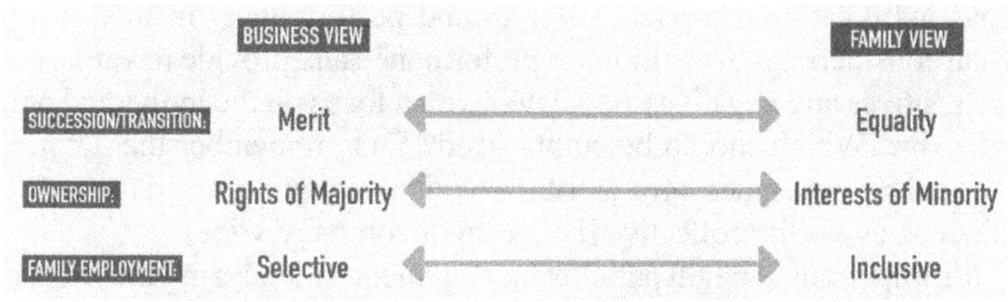


**Figure 1.4** *Common paradoxes in family business*

It's important to keep in mind that family businesses would not be so successful if they contained only differences – though these tend to stand out because of their often dramatic nature and the challenges they pose. The business can be adapted to meet the needs of the family, as discussed earlier with the banking family; specifically, multiple features of businesses (such as geography and structure) can be customized to the interests and competencies of family members. At the same time, the family contributes strength to the business by bringing to it a special set of values and traditions. For example, family members bring vigilance and passion to the business, because they are deeply invested in the business' success. The family and the business also have the same goals with respect to continuity: the family wants to see the business carried on, not so much for the current shareholders, but for future generations of the family.

## PARADOX OF INDIVIDUAL *AND* COLLECTIVE

Having looked at possible areas of strength and conflict between the family and business systems, now consider some of the typical ways a family business might encounter a paradox in its daily operation. One paradox often present on a day-to-day basis is the struggle between performance and rewards for the individual *and* performance and rewards for the group or organization. Which is more important to reward: the achievements of the individual or the group?

Of course this individual-versus-group issue is one all organizations face. Yet the challenge is heightened in family businesses because the group is typically not a collection of unrelated individuals, but family members. From the family's point of view, members are all equal; from the business's point of view, individuals can be differentiated based on their qualifications, services offered, and performance. In this context, when considering how to monitor performance and provide rewards, there are positives and negatives associated with a focus on the individual or the collective. Which should be emphasized? First, remember the definition of paradox: both sides have merit. Individual recognition and rewards are valuable, as are the collective (i.e., team or company-wide).

It's important to begin paradox management by analyzing the two sides involved – in this case, the individual *and* the group. In some ways they are mirror images – it appears initially that making a choice that is a positive for the individual is likely a negative for the group, and a decision that is a negative for the individual may well be a positive for the group.

For example, if the choice is to emphasize the group, the fallout may be several people (such as freeloaders or social loafers) who don't meet their individual responsibilities; as a result, others have to pick up the slack, which can ultimately lead to new problems and conflicts. The opposite is true when the individual is emphasized. In this case, each individual may meet their own individual obligations, but no one is looking out for what the group collectively produces, and the group may fail to meet its overarching responsibilities. So choosing one side or the other does not yield optimal long-term results. Instead, it is necessary to choose both the individual *and* the group.

First, accept the paradox for what it is, and seek to gain the greatest value from both sides. In other words, work with the tension between the two opposing perspectives in the paradox of individual *and* group to capture the energy from both.

Identify the positives of focusing on the individual and the positives of focusing on the group and then reinforce both the individual *and* the group in organizational traditions, values, policies and processes. In doing so, the organization will have gained the capability to reap the best from both – by strengthening the individual, the group is strengthened, and by strengthening the group, the individual is strengthened. Each reinforces the other, as depicted in Figure 1.5. In a discussion with a group of family business professionals on a similar topic, the following phrase emerged to capture this particular paradox: "The strength of the wolf is in the pack."

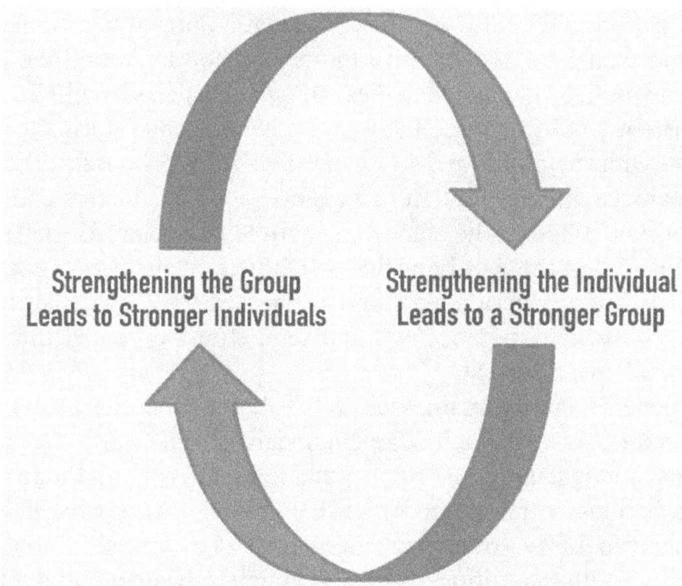


**Figure 1.5** *Individual* and *collective paradox*

## INDIVIDUAL *AND* COLLECTIVE IN ACTION

How might emphasizing both play out in a specific family business scenario? A Spanish client in the metalworking industry was introducing the next generation, his nephew, into the business with a job in production. Given the nephew's personality, education, experiences, and interests, the family saw him as a likely future CEO of the company.

The challenge was how to support the nephew's role in the production environment while allowing him time to learn about broader aspects of the company. Overemphasizing his personal development might have sacrificed the goals of the production team, including building a quality product and delivering it on time. At the same time, ensuring his exposure to multiple areas within the company was important to his evolution into a capable future leader and the future of the business itself.

The company's answer was to develop the structures and processes to enable him to do both. To ensure success the CEO communicated the plan to the rest of the organization, *and* supported it with resources that would enable success all around. Specifically, the nephew took on a production role, and it was acknowledged upfront that 80 percent of his time would be dedicated to the production team and the other 20 percent would be dedicated to "learning the business," including joining the current CEO (his uncle) at board meetings and on trips to the field to meet with customers and suppliers. This solution allowed the production team, including the CEO's nephew, to be productive and meet its obligations, while at the same time providing a plan for developing a future leader of the family business. Ultimately, the nephew succeeded – both on the production team and as the next CEO – due largely to the skills, confidence, perspective, and reputation he gained through this Both/*AND* arrangement.

In general, family businesses are well positioned to master paradox management, as it is a fundamental part of who and what they are: they have longstanding, regular practice identifying and managing the contradictions within paradoxes. This practice can evolve into a deep internal capability to manage paradoxes. In turn, this competence, combined with a traditions-based approach to business, and a focus on the long term, can yield a competitive advantage that helps explain why family businesses thrive across generations. It's likely that the capability to see both sides of paradoxical problems is a strong driver of business adaptability and innovation.

## CELEBRATING PARADOX AT BERETTA

Family businesses that are successful across generations intuitively manage paradox-based contradictions well. Paradox management has become an integral part of their history. A great example of this is the Beretta Company, a global gun and accessory manufacturer founded in 1526 and still run by the family 14 generations later.[2] The company's motto is engraved on the family's coat of arms and hangs proudly in company offices: "Prudence and Audacity."

> Prudence – wise in practical matters
> *AND*
> Audacity – fearlessly daring

The Beretta family business motto, at the heart of the business for nearly 500 years, is the epitome of paradox. The notion of "Prudence and Audacity" also pervades many other elements of the company's approach, including an emphasis on "systematic creativity." What does this mean in a practical sense? How can a company be both prudent *and* audacious – and systematic *and* creative – at the same time? What does this mean for its day-to-day operations?

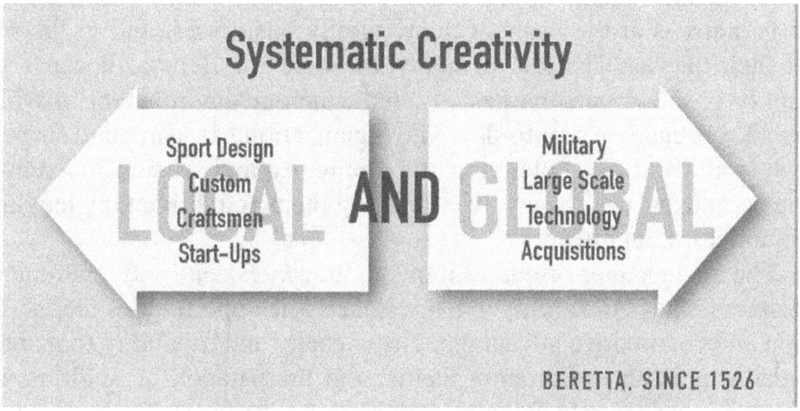


**Figure 1.6** *Beretta's paradoxes in action*

These paradoxes play out in multiple ways within Beretta. The company and family are tremendously proud of their centuries-old traditions, yet constantly search for new ways of doing things. Located in a small town in the mountains, the Beretta offices have a museum-like quality, with original wooden floors beneath the desks and history-rich pictures on the walls; at the same time, the operations turn out some of the industry's most innovative products. They offer two broad product lines: high-volume, mass-produced military weapons and custom-designed, handcrafted sports guns. In the factory where their products are made, assembly-line robots labor alongside craftspeople engraving pieces by hand. Beretta also seeks to grow both organically (in other words, based on core products) and through acquisition.

As a company, Beretta is full of these paradoxes. What really ferments the company's strategic change and evolution – and serves as the underlying engine of innovation and creativity – is living every day with these paradoxes.

This global company housed in a remote village exemplifies several adages: "Eyes on the past, yet focus on the future" and "Run the business with your heart and your money," among others. Inside Beretta, these inherent contradictions percolate … percolate … percolate … and ultimately spark new ideas, opportunities, and insights that drive the next set of successes. Today, Beretta – the oldest manufacturing company in the world – employs over 2,600 people and is a leading innovator in the industry.

Paradox is at the heart of many family businesses, and in the soul of their success. This is certainly the case for Beretta, because the family business persona has fostered a unique environment in which paradoxes can live day-to-day. The organization has learned to suspend judgment, not only tolerating the ambiguity and tension inherent to the paradoxes, but ultimately embracing them and thriving by handling paradoxes thoughtfully.

The next chapter discusses more about *why* Beretta and other family businesses have the ability to harness strategic opportunities for adaptation and competitive advantage. The capacity and capability to manage paradoxes is an overarching theme, and the paradox of tradition and change is the central challenge, and opportunity, for family businesses.

## ASSESSMENT SUMMARY

At this time it might be beneficial to return to the Family First–Business First Assessment introduced at the beginning of Part I and study your own results. Appendix C contains detailed instructions for completing and scoring the assessment.

The purpose of this assessment is to provide family members with a snapshot of their individual and collective perspectives on fundamental business-first and family-first issues. The survey becomes a starting point for discussion among family members about why people responded one way or another, especially when responses diverge. Discussion of the survey results can help family members establish a common platform for approaching these tricky issues, largely by de-emphasizing the emotional and personal nature of conflicts and seeing them as more situational or structural. This, in turn fosters family and business success – especially through appreciating the consequences of emphasizing a given approach over another.

# 2 Tradition *and* Change in Family Firms

Stockholm-based Axel Johnson, Inc, traces its roots in the shipping and trading business all the way back to 1873. As suggested by the quote below, tradition *and* change is a central theme for the company.

> The group [company] contains meetings between old and new, past and present, experience and curiosity, long-term perspective and eagerness.[1]
>
> Axel Johnson AB

Business-owning families invest generations of blood, sweat, and tears into their growth and development, from the founding generation to the current leadership. As they seek ways to successfully combine the love of the family with the profit motive of the business, family businesses worldwide face paradoxes from their inception. Paradoxes are embedded, deeply, in the very DNA of their firms. The need to wrestle with paradoxes helps both families and businesses become stronger and more resilient.

The tradition *and* change paradox challenges all family businesses, especially during times of transition. Whether the firm is located in Chennai (India), Chiapas (Mexico), or Cheyenne (Wyoming), every family business that survives across the generations has to address this universal paradox.

Each generation must decide what to preserve from the past, and what to let go. Major issues – such as whether or not to continue manufacturing the business's original product, where to locate operating facilities, or how large a workforce to maintain – force the family business into challenging discussions regarding tradition *and* change. But even small issues related to this paradox can cause conflicts: which color to paint the building's entryway, what painting to hang in the president's office, or what photograph to print on the business's holiday card, for instance.

The traditions that evolve represent much more than meets the eye. Families may know that they need to adapt in order to survive, but this is more easily understood than executed. So how can the paradox of tradition *and* change best be managed? What can be learned from family businesses that manage the paradox in exemplary ways?

## THE GODREJ GROUP: A MODEL OF TRADITION *AND* CHANGE

Family businesses that acknowledge the paradox of tradition *and* change have a strong appreciation for their roots. They understand and honor the founding family's longstanding traditions and values. At the same time, the businesses have continued to evolve to meet the needs of their current environments. How is this possible? Because, rather than abandoning the old to take on the new, they are both honoring *and* holding high the core traditions established by the company's founders *and* using these to promote innovation amidst new challenges.

A great example of living this paradox of tradition and change is the Godrej Group, a successful, five-generation, consumer goods family business in India. They "aim to achieve a model mix of tradition *and* innovation." According to a Godrej family executive, "We are traditional in terms of trust, integrity and employee welfare, but as modernity and innovations are extremely important, we like to absorb the latest developments." So how does this play out on a day-to-day basis within Godrej? Consider the following element of the company's corporate governance structure:

> The division of two important committees perhaps best demonstrates how these divergent concepts of tradition *and* innovation (change) can sit side by side in a modern family-owned business. The group's corporate governance committee is overseen by a think-tank of senior people who analyze geopolitical issues; while an executive committee of "bright young things" aged 30–40 provides dynamic and innovative ideas to improve the business.[2]

The Godrej Group embraces and provides a role for those who have lived through many decades of changes in the business, in politics, and in the environment. Given their intimate knowledge of the past, they have the perspective to understand how shifts and trends in these interrelated domains might play out within their customer base, with their competition's potential response, with their employees, and across the company as a whole. This senior group's view is then juxtaposed with that of the younger generation, which may have a stronger sense of the current business context, rapid market changes, and greater familiarity with relevant technological advances. In this way, Godrej benefits from both the history-based insights *and* the forward-facing perspective within its walls: tradition *and* change.

In the context of the Godrej Group example, consider several characteristics of family firms that help them to both protect the sources of their past success *and*, at the same time, seek needed innovation. After considerable research and reflection, four characteristics – unique to family businesses – have been identified as playing important roles in this regard:

- distinctive time orientation
- complex successor dilemmas
- internally driven strategy
- enduring values

## DISTINCTIVE TIME ORIENTATION

Studies of family businesses' perspective on time show that, relative to non-family firms, their top management's time orientation is more focused on both the past *and* the future than the present (see Figure 2.1). In contrast, top management teams of non-family firms are much more focused on the present.[3]

A management team with a greater orientation to the past brings experience of and perspective on history to problems and decisions. Such a team also tends to create more measured forecasts of both potential *and* risk than present-oriented groups. A more future-oriented team tends to approach problems with greater patience and more "options-based" thinking; thus they keep the door to new information

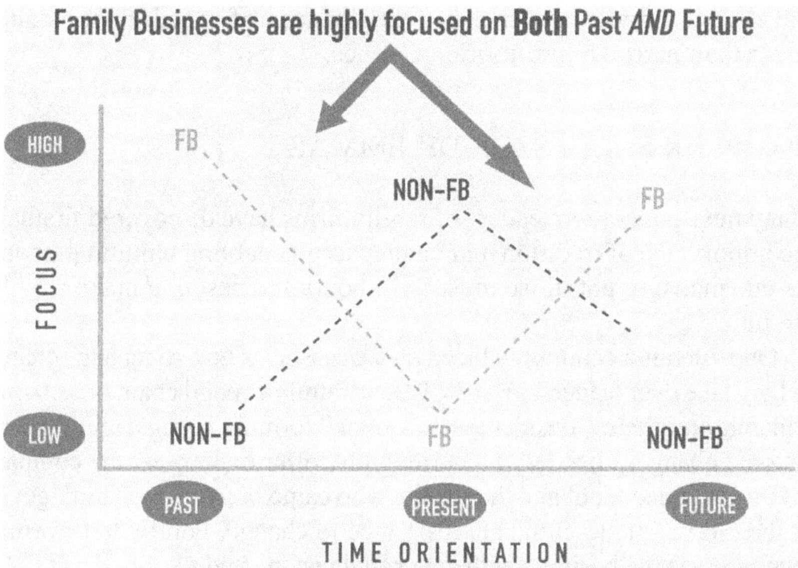


**Figure 2.1** *Time orientation of top management in family firms compared with public firms*

and new possibilities more open than a present-oriented team might. A strong orientation to the present generally leads to more speculative risks and returns and is associated with overconfidence in judgment regarding implementation of change.[4]

The following quote suggests that it's hard to overstate the effects of time orientation on management beliefs and behavior:

> There is no more powerful, pervasive influence on how individuals think and cultures interact than different perspectives on time – the more we mentally partition time into past, present, future.[5]
>
> Gonzalez and Zimbardo

In this context, it's worth exploring the benefits of a long-term view for a family business a bit further. If the time horizon is long, potentially disabling contradictions are more likely to melt away. In addition, with a long-term view, more subjective factors can enter problem solving and decision making, increasing the chances of broader approaches, rather than narrowly profit-oriented ones.

## COMPLEX SUCCESSOR DILEMMAS

Many next-generation leaders of family firms have discovered firsthand the importance of tradition *and* change as an enabling cultural paradox. As one manager put it, we must both honor the past *and* make way for the future.

One dilemma commonly faced by successors is how to manage change as they take over leadership – as CEO, as family council chair, or as family philanthropy chair. Consider the "textbook" formula for managing organizational change: First, build a burning platform: make clear the company is in crisis. Second, blame the people who came before you. Third, get rid of the old regime to eliminate resistance to change. Fourth, transform or revolutionize the business with a personal vision. And so on.

Now apply this model to nearly any family business succession or transition scenario. Here's how the steps above might translate:

- First – "Our situation is horrible."
- Second – "Mom and Dad are responsible."
- Third – "Everyone – aunts, uncles, siblings – who's been in the organization for the last 25 years must go."
- Fourth – "I have compelling answers for how to transform the business."

The textbook method clearly doesn't work for family businesses. Yet any successor – in family business or elsewhere – faces the challenge of driving change. The organization often requires change to continue to succeed. At the same time, the organization is steeped in tradition, and in many cases the previous leader is still very present and often viewed as a hero. So how does a family business successor say, "I value the past, I honor and appreciate the past," *and* "We need to change," at the same time?

To compound matters, the successor often seeks to make a sizable initial impact, sometimes because the rest of the organization might be thinking that she or he has ascended to a leadership role for the wrong reasons. Although the motivation to drive results can be grounded in a desire for positive organizational growth, it may also be motivated by the potentially misguided, more emotionally driven need to prove oneself. The successor, then, needs to have sufficient self-confidence to avoid leading an ego-driven revolution in favor of guiding a more thoughtful initial course of action focused on continuity and anchored firmly in the organization's traditions. Only with this foundation in place can the successor introduce change effectively.

This focus on tradition allows the broader organization to recognize that the company's past success rests on a foundation of fundamental values and traditions, rather than a set of specific, prescribed practices. For example, the company may see clearly that their approach to pricing is based on a long-standing philosophy, not a simple policy of always up-charging 20 percent. The message of tradition *and* change can also be reinforced by preceding generations, who might say, "Keep the values of the past alive in the organization, but recognize that our practices will have to evolve to ensure future success." Values derive power from their endurance. Practices must change with the times.

Observations of effective transitions within family businesses suggest that many successors find ways to both honor the past *and* promote change for the future. The specific message by which they convey this is then used repeatedly within the organization to reinforce the paradox of tradition *and* change. Figure 2.2 presents examples of such messages.

***"My goal is to build on our tradition of change."***

***"I want to remind everyone that innovation is our tradition."***

***"Our Legacy of Innovation."***

***"Our Motto: New Ideas; Old Ideals."***

***"Preserve the Best; Reinvent the Rest."***

***"Tradition is not history. Tradition is eternity."***

***"We embrace both tradition and the modern way of doing things."***

***"Always changing to remain the same."***

***"Green grows organically amongst the gold."***

**Figure 2.2** *Successors' statements of tradition and change*

The phrases in Figure 2.2 serve as examples of successors honoring what has come before without stagnating in it. The levels of patience and strategic foresight represented by the statements are critical to making tradition *and* change truly live and breathe within any family business. The thoughtful successor emphasizes tradition and other stated values as the cornerstone for future success, reinforcing the foundation built by previous generations and helping the business draw upon this for the strength to promote future success.

Appreciating paradox is not likely to be natural for new successors. Embracing ambiguity and uncertainty is rarely comfortable, for anyone. In fact, acknowledging paradox probably competes with a new successor's instincts to appear clear, decisive, and in charge. The idea of seeking to manage paradox may also contradict some popular notions of leadership: "You must have a compelling, simple vision," for example. Most rising leaders have also focused on learning algorithmic problem-solving and decision-making processes, which they rely on for confidence and persuasiveness. Yet next-generation successors can benefit deeply from making explicit how to identify and manage paradoxes. One high-profile father to a successor-in-waiting said it as follows:

> Change does not change tradition. It strengthens it. Change is a challenge and an opportunity; not a threat.[6]
>
> Prince Philip, Duke of Edinburgh

## INTERNALLY DRIVEN STRATEGY

As described in the Berretta case in Chapter 1, the company prospers from accepting contradicting strategies and processes: hand-crafted and mass-produced, local and global presence, organic growth and acquisition-based growth, among others. Beretta has been at this so long that these strategic contradictions often become the origins of their new and evolving strategies. Emerging from their loyal workforce, their extraordinarily strong culture, their family "DNA," and tradition of leadership by family members, Beretta's strategies are internally generated, sparked by paradoxical tensions, and filtered by their values.

This strategy-formulation process is unconventional, yet not uncommon in family firms. Most strategic planning processes look for ideas and opportunities from “outside” – from market changes or competitive moves, for example. The company then aligns its culture, leadership selection, and employee training to the strategy after the fact. In contrast, successful family firms generate adaptive strategies from the “inside,” developing strategic approaches that are already consistent with their competencies and culture. Put simply, who they are drives what they become, as opposed to what they seek shaping how they operate. Figure 2.3 depicts this contrast.

**Figure 2.3** *Traditional strategy compared with family business strategy formulation*

As an example, a family business owned several plastics manufacturing plants in the United States in the early 1970s. They had perfected a philosophy of management – focused on engaging employees and customers in process improvement programs – that they believed might be universal. The family also had a passion for world travel, and thus relished the thought of doing business in different cultures. Turning curiosity into action, a family member took a job in Belgium with one of the firm’s suppliers. Soon afterward, the family indulged their cross-cultural interest further by purchasing a European manufacturer. Several decades later, this family business emerged as the global leader in its industry. The family had followed a specific passion they shared

– rather than addressing a documented, quantifiable market need – and ultimately positioned the business for large-scale success. Currently, a next-generation family member is studying in Singapore. We can predict the next continent for growth.

As stated earlier, Beretta also exemplifies this inside-out approach to strategy. For the gun-maker, the arrival of new leadership (in each successive generation), rather than significant market shifts, tended to herald new business strategies. But these were not strategies based on whim or leaders' idiosyncrasies; rather, they evolved from the character of the company, its values, its history, its leadership, and its environment. In fact, it can be argued that most new strategies in old family firms are not really new: they already exist as concepts and fragments; in its own way, each new generation of leadership takes them on, champions them, and adapts them to market conditions.

## ENDURING VALUES

Contradictions and paradoxes within a firm's culture bring more wisdom to problem solving, more balance to analyzing alternatives, more potential to possibilities, and more care to risk taking. The values an organization embodies or professes to have also affect its potential to welcome and manage paradoxes. Consider two sets of values. Values like those on the left-hand side in Figure 2.4 are more transactional and measurable, and are associated with more algorithmic problem-solving approaches.

**Figure 2.4** *Values comparison*

The list on the left of Figure 2.4 represents very common values in "professionally managed" organizations, or prototypical public companies. They lend themselves to tight operations and a strong orientation to results. On the other hand, they don't represent the history of the company, nor do these values ease people's discomfort during times of ambiguity and uncertainty. Further, they don't provide insight into the integration or synthesis of paradoxical problems. Next consider the values in the right-hand column of Figure 2.4.

Such values, far more common in family businesses, are likely rooted in a business's founding days and context, rather than crafted subsequently; they emerge from the founder's or founding group's spirit and personality, rather than being drafted by committee. They are also more "human" in nature, giving comfort during difficult and uncertain times, and providing more security and stability during change. Note also that the values in the right column typically drive their more transactional counterpart values on the left side (hence the left-facing arrows).

It is interesting to consider how these unique family business values support management of the tradition *and* change paradox. The very personal and individual values of a family firm often lead to a more direct connection between individuals and the firm. This vibrant connection – combined with humility – supports the next generation's commitment to the lessons of the past. A next generation that is passionate about preserving the past, can also be adamant about needing adaptation and innovation for the future. The family value of courage supports the next generation as they pursue this challenging Both/*AND* approach. In this way, family values can play an important role in managing tradition *and* change.

As an additional example, consider the cultural values of the large, third-generation consumer-foods family firm Strauss in Israel. It is clear that these three statements would be very helpful in managing the tension between tradition and change across the generations:

Daring *and* Caring
Passion *and* Responsibility
Teamwork *and* Each Person Counts

## TRADITION *AND* CHANGE AT BERETTA

Beretta expresses its approach to tradition *and* change as "evolution *and* innovation." This paradox is perhaps the most important characteristic of the firm's culture. Respecting tradition gives people a stable platform for understanding the "right thing to do" and carrying it out with confidence. At the same time, appreciating change or innovation helps the organization stay relevant and do new things. The paradox of evolution *and* innovation helps Beretta move forward without losing sight of what came before, all part of the company's overarching motto of "Prudence *and* Audacity."

Table 2.1 illustrates how Beretta has demonstrated the four characteristics needed for exemplary management of the paradox of tradition *and* change. The first characteristic is time orientation. As Beretta attended to the challenges of the present, it still showed focused attention on both the past *and* the future. This focus on both can be seen clearly in its approach to business locations. Beretta's corporate headquarters remain in the small town of Gardone, Italy, where the enterprise began and much of the continued expertise in gun-making resides. While maintaining this facility is seen as essential to continuity, it has not stopped Beretta from building new facilities in the United States as a statement of its commitment to creating capacity for enduring global growth.

The second characteristic is successor dilemmas. As each succes-

**Table 2.1** *Beretta: management of tradition* and *change*

| **Family business characteristics** | **How each generation values tradition *and* change at Beretta** |
|---|---|
| Distinctive time orientation | Cherish the headquarters in Gardone, Italy *and* Launch Beretta USA |
| Successor dilemmas | Sustain historical product line *and* Expand product offerings |
| Internally driven strategy | Preserve purely artisanal work *and* Initiate large-scale, high-tech production |
| Enduring values | "Culture is in the walls here. It becomes part of you with each breath … something common to everyone in this company, something shared, yet unspoken." |

*Source:* John L. Ward and Colleen Lief, *IMD–3–1495 Prudence and audacity: The house of Beretta*, International Institute for Management Development, v. 21.02.2005, 2005.

sive generation of family management assumed leadership, they found a way to both value their forebears' achievements while making their own mark. This is demonstrated profoundly in the evolution of Beretta's product line over time. With great skill, each generation of family management was able to maintain the appeal of their hand-crafted products while introducing new products in response to market opportunities. For example, in recent years, Beretta started an apparel line to complement its offerings.

The third characteristic is internally driven strategy. Over decades, Beretta has placed value on the artisanal production methods of their earliest years. For this company, the phrase "This is how we've always done it" is not a statement of resistance to change, but a celebration of proven accomplishment. And it exists alongside an equally celebrated commitment to applying large-scale, technologically advanced production approaches. Each approach is appreciated, celebrated, and applied appropriately. For example, in the early decades of the 1900s, Beretta prospered by developing a military product line, which has succeeded and expanded since then.

The fourth and final characteristic regarding the tradition *and* change paradox is enduring values. Beretta has been able to develop new and improved strategies from among its range of seemingly contradictory values and activities. What allows these strategy-related ideas to germinate and gather momentum is the organization's culture. A simple "black and white" culture is unlikely to supply the oxygen to bring many diverse ideas to life. But if the culture (as well as the strategic activity) includes paradoxical thinking, then it will accommodate new possibilities more easily. And these new ideas can be shaped to carry the family business's distinctiveness – rather than merely being evaluated against financial criteria.

Beretta's culture leverages both craftsmanship *and* robotics because it values the past and is focused on the future. Beretta fosters the ideas and passions of individual employees – in service of corporate goals – because its culture champions personal freedom *and* personal responsibility. The key paradoxes that comprise Beretta's cultural values – which are also more humanistic in nature – are summarized in Figure 2.5.

Consider the cultural value of "personal responsibility," or what's known as the "Power of One" at Beretta. This value is intended to both

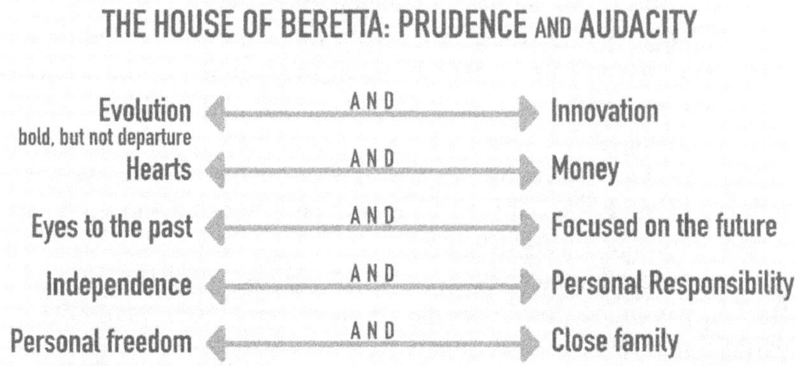


**Figure 2.5** *Beretta cultural components*

*Source:* John L. Ward and Colleen Lief, *IMD–3–1495 Prudence and audacity: The house of Beretta*, International Institute for Management Development, v. 21.02.2005, 2005.

empower individual employees and hold them personally accountable for the welfare of the organization. By creating what might be thought of as "controlled entrepreneurship," it promotes a non-bureaucratic and highly efficient environment.

This chapter acquainted us with an array of Enterprising Families that have grown and prospered across many generations, achieving the ultimate goal of continuity. In order to survive and thrive across the years, these family businesses had to learn to foster both tradition *and* change. Those that mastered this skill now serve as examples to other family firms, showing that it is not necessary to choose one to the exclusion of the other, but that both tradition *and* change are needed for long-term prosperity of both the family *and* the business.

# Part II

# Identifying Both

Perpetuating the family business is the ultimate management challenge. What do you have to do to be successful? Two deceptively simple things:

- You must keep the business strong enough and healthy enough to last into the next generation.
- You must continue a healthy family into the next generation.

What's more, when either challenge would be more than enough to deal with by itself, you have to manage both of these Herculean tasks at the same time.

When you try to manage both – as you must – you quickly discover the many contradictions that are inherent when a family and a business are locked together in a unit that we call a family firm.

The dilemmas a business-owning family faces, meanwhile, are epitomized in a question we have heard over and over:

> Why can't we have a family business and a happy family at the same time?[1]
>
> John Ward

*This page intentionally left blank*

# 3 Predictable Paradoxes Across the Generations

Family business paradoxes emerge predictably during transitions from one generation to the next in both the family *and* the business.

> Typically, the rapacity and acquisitive focus of the first generation gives way to the cautious, conservative ethos of the second and the spoiled and heedless frivolity of the third.[1]
>
> Adam Bellow, *In Praise of Nepotism*

> I must study politics and war that my sons may have liberty to study . . . mathematics and philosophy, geography, natural history, naval architecture, navigation, commerce and agriculture in order to give their children a right to study paintings, poetry, music, architecture, statuary, tapestry and porcelain.[2]
>
> John Adams, Paris, 1778

When the Bancroft family sold Dow Jones & Company to Rupert Murdoch's News Corporation in 2007, it was the logical consequence of a long-standing business-first approach to their enterprise. Family members had been noticeably absent from the management and governance of the company for decades. In a letter to fellow family members, Crawford Hill wrote, "We are actually now paying the price for our passivity over the past 25 years."[3] For several decades, little effort was made to educate or involve family shareholders in meaningful ways. We might say that an inability to manage the family first *and* business first paradox at the *Wall Street Journal* led to its eventual sale. And we might predict that if Rupert Murdoch doesn't combine a healthy respect for both family *and* business, his company will also not survive as a family enterprise.

## GENERATIONAL OSCILLATION

Family business paradoxes emerge predictably during transitions from one generation to the next in both the family and the business. Along the way, as the business and family grow and develop, each generation faces a new set of dynamics and demands. Although each family business is unique, at each stage of development they confront many of the same challenges and opportunities, and thus the generation involved in that stage tends to develop similar priorities. For example, what is important to the founding generation is similar across geographic locations and industries. Sibling partnerships face similar challenges across sectors, and tend to make the same kinds of choices in response. In the third generation, cousin collaborations in family businesses worldwide are called upon to master a predictable set of challenges, and they tend to respond in ways that bear more similarities than differences.

Within these predictable generational dynamics are predictable paradoxes. Each generational set of paradoxes results from the common set of challenges that face businesses and families as they grow and develop over time. Figure 3.1 depicts the generational pattern described.

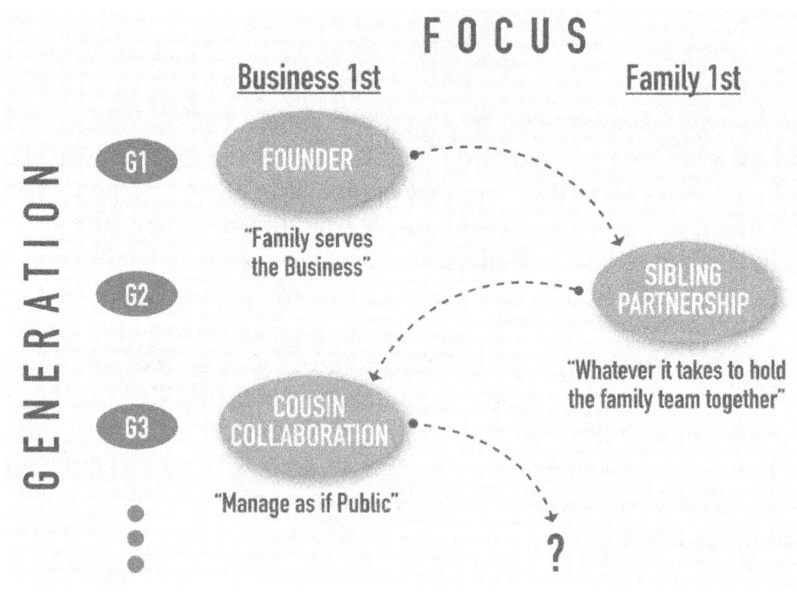


**Figure 3.1** *Oscillation in family business focus across generations*

Founding Stage (G1) businesses are usually business first, to promote the business' survival and success. Siblings grow up in an environment that tends to prioritize business needs over those of the family. Not surprisingly, this leads in the Sibling Partnership Stage (G2) to a reasserting of family needs, in an attempt to counterbalance the founding generation's business-first focus. The second generation often has the luxury of taking a more family-first stance, because it can rely on the reputation and customer base the founding generation created. There is also a financial incentive for the family to stay together, as it's very difficult for one or two individuals to afford purchasing 25 percent, 33 percent, or 50 percent of the business in the form of their siblings' stock (if one or more siblings opt to depart).

As the business moves into the third generation, the focus tends to cycle back to business first, but in a different way than in the Founding Stage. Most likely, the family business is now owned by a larger, more diverse group of cousins, siblings, trusts, and possibly some non-family shareholders as well. The cousins are often dispersed geographically. They may not even know each other well, and only a few of them may be sufficiently interested and/or skilled to work in the business.

The diversity and complexity of this Cousin Collaboration Stage creates plenty of family and ownership challenges – and corresponding paradoxes. Further, in this stage there is usually pressure to professionalize operations. These factors combine to create a natural impetus to trade the G2 family-first focus for a G3 business-first focus. Although this stage echoes the Founding Stage, it is with a different emphasis: astute family businesses have learned by the third generation that an over-emphasis on family or business is ill-advised. Thus they seek to maintain attention, resources and emphasis upon both family *and* business. As noted in Chapter 1, family businesses that successfully make this transition may be considered Enterprising Families. (More on that at the end of this chapter.)

The tendency to cycle family business focus from generation to generation is well documented. When this natural oscillation takes an extreme form, it can be traumatic. On the other hand, because these dynamics are quite predictable, the swing in focus from business first to family first can be anticipated and actively managed. In fact, when well managed, these paradoxes can lead to synthesis, or simultaneous pursuit of both sides – family *and* business – and superior performance. This chapter examines the predictable paradoxes that accompany each generation of a family business showing how business families typically respond to each, and how they might move toward managing them more effectively.

## PREDICTABLE PARADOXES: FOUNDER STAGE

As the name suggests, the Founding Stage is a first-generation phenomenon. But sometimes the *dynamic* of the stage does not emerge until the second or even third generation of a business family. For example, great home builders often emerge from early generations of carpenters; large medical firms evolve from families of doctors. The dynamic of the Founding Stage is typically one of tremendous vision and risk, of creating something new and significant. The stage is most often associated with one powerful and talented individual, but can also be expressed by energetic and visionary partnerships or even groups. The stage also includes several predictable paradoxes, which are brought to life next, through the example of a specific family business.

### Meet George and Suzanne Sample and Sample Transportation

This case study is based on an actual family business; specific facts have been disguised.

Born in a small town in central Colorado in 1918, George Sample was an inquisitive, intelligent young man with a love for anything on wheels. He spent his early years working alongside his father, repairing bicycles and farm equipment in the garage behind the house. George's aspirations quickly outgrew his father's small backyard business: he began to work for the local car repair shop during the day while earning his high-school degree at night. By age 23, George married his long-time sweetheart, Suzanne, and opened his own repair shop in the center of town. Sample Automotive, their business, was destined to become one of Colorado's largest family enterprises.

During the 1940s, George and Suzanne kept very busy in their respective realms of business and family. George was rarely home, giving every ounce of his attention and energy to expanding the business. Over the next two decades, Sample Automotive grew from an auto repair shop, to a car, truck, and farm equipment repair business, to an automotive leasing business, all the while taking advantage of real estate and property investment opportunities. In the early 1960s the business was renamed Sample Transportation.

Alongside the expansion of the firm, Suzanne nurtured the expansion of the Sample family. She worked hard to create a warm and secure environment for the four Sample children: George Jr., Geri, Suzi, and Louis. She insisted that the entire family eat dinner together each evening, gathering around the kitchen table in the family home, which had been built behind the business offices.

## Founder Stage: business paradoxes

Like many founders, George liked to be in control. He strove to hire hard-working employees, but gave his trust begrudgingly. For example, he required all important decisions to pass through him. Even after the business became quite large and geographically dispersed, George found it difficult to share significant information or decision making with employees, regardless of their skills or loyalty. This management style left George perpetually exhausted and burdened. Paradoxically, George would likely have created a stronger business by giving up some control and placing more trust in others. He failed to recognize the paradox of control *and* trust, and did not appreciate that its two sides were not opposites but mutually supportive elements. Had George learned to trust others more and share responsibility with them, he might have built an even stronger organization.

Nonetheless, George's hard work, vision, and appetite for risk were great advantages in the business's early years, as was his talent for finding and capitalizing on opportunities. In general, he showed a strong preference for expedience over patience. His focus on growth led him to make decisions quickly, rather than gathering more information, which sometimes meant having to make subsequent adjustments or "clean up messes." George failed to see that a more measured approach could result in faster progress.

George's disdain for research – a characteristic of many founders – was part of his approach to the paradox of action *and* planning. By seeing planning as a threat to rapid advancement, rather than a foundation for sustainable progress, George led his company to take a "Ready – Fire – Aim" approach, bristling at attempts to document policies or procedures. Established systems, he felt, would hamper the business's ability to respond to emergent opportunities. "We'll have our heads buried so far inside our desks that we won't be looking around at what's really happening in the world," he was known to say. He saw the two complementary sides of the paradox of action *and* planning as mutually exclusive. If he could have recognized the need for both, he would have been pleased to see how planning often leads to enhanced activity. Also, he would have seen how an action orientation leads to more effective planning. Taking a Both/*AND* approach to the action *and* planning paradox would likely have helped George build an even stronger and more sustainable organization for the next generation.

In fact, George had strong ambitions to pass the business to his children. Yet, when faced with the paradox of proprietorship *and* stewardship, he consistently focused on proprietorship. He emphasized taking advantage of opportunities of the moment, rather than building capability for the future. Although Sample Transportation had substantial size and scope by then, George approached its leadership as if it were still a one-man shop. He kept his hands on everything, and resisted planning and entrusting others. The company relied upon George for all decisions, large and small. Ironically, because of this, decision making in Sample Transportation's ostensibly seize-the-opportunity culture became quite slow. Hampered by its dependence on George, the organization had limited flexibility, with increasing difficulty in responding to unexpected developments.

With greater awareness of the paradoxes he was grappling with, George might have recognized how his preference for expedience and control was actually threatening the organization's long-term survival. Rather than seeing carefully planned systems and procedures (part of a stewardship orientation) as slowing things down, he might have recognized these as enhancing the company's ability to respond expediently for the long term.

## Founder Stage: family paradoxes

Suzanne didn't realize it, but she also was facing predictable paradoxes in the founding stage of her own domain: the family. One of the most common paradoxes that all families (business and non-business) face is that of roots *and* wings. Healthy families provide both by giving their children a solid sense of grounding, and simultaneously encouraging them to explore the world independently, to learn about, test, and strengthen their individual abilities. A typical mistake that Founding Stage families make, then, is emphasizing roots over wings.

Consider the Sample family. Growing up, George had enjoyed tremendous freedom. That freedom permitted him to build his initial small businesses, the precursors to the larger-scale Sample Transportation. Yet it appeared that George had forgotten the benefits of this early experience. Just as he sought to make and oversee all business decisions, he exerted tremendous control within the family, leading to an extreme focus on roots over wings.

Family trips and vacations were practically nonexistent, as George couldn't break away from the business. He also had few interests, hobbies, or activities that were not related to the business. For example, while he enjoyed fishing with customers at the local trout stream, he never took the time to go with the children, and lacked the patience to fish alone. To get an early start at the office, George went to bed early each night, rather than spending time at home, or in outside activities with the family, or socializing with friends. As a result, the children stayed close to home, playing together in the large backyard. Once George Jr. and Geri, the two eldest, could read and write, George took them to the office most Saturdays. There, they played together all day long, making up games associated with the business (and using lots of office supplies).

By high school, there was no question that George Jr. and Geri would work at the business. George Jr. helped out in the shop, although he didn't appear to have his father's natural talent for cars. He idolized his father and cherished their time together. Geri filed business documents and answered the phones. A quick study, she was very good with numbers: fast and accurate. Seeing this, Sample Transportation's accounting manager took her under his wing, showing her the basics of the firm's accounting and payment practices. The two elder children enjoyed becoming part of the business, and Suzanne, their mother, was very happy to see them spend time with their father.

## Founder Stage: summary

Figure 3.2 summarizes the fundamental paradoxes found at Sample Transportation and most family businesses during the G1 or Founding Stage. Although the family is appreciated and valued during this phase, the overall strategy is clearly business first. The founder usually has a crystal-clear vision of the future that he can't pursue quickly enough, and prefers action over planning. This action orientation leads to swiftly made decisions, emphasizing expediency over patience. Because he is driven by his personal vision (often the source of tremendous success), the founder tends to favor control over trust, preferring to do everything himself. This control can yield tremendous results, but clearly creates problems when taken to an extreme.

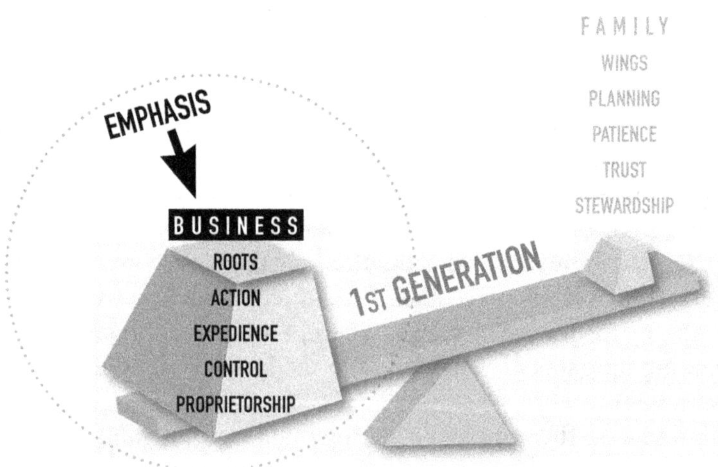


**Figure 3.2** *Founder Stage fundamental paradoxes*

Ironically, the founder is typically more of a proprietor than a steward: he is more focused on near-term results and problem solving, to the detriment of systems and structures necessary to perpetuate the business in the longer term. And finally, in the family realm, the tendency toward control takes the form of an emphasis on roots over wings. All of these paradoxes are characterized by two sides, one of which the founder prefers strongly over the other. When the preferred value is pursued to the exclusion of its counterpart, predictable problems emerge. If the Sample family had been more knowledgeable about paradoxes in family businesses, they might have more deliberately emphasized both sides of the paradox.

As demonstrated by the Sample family example, G1, the first generation tends to be business first. During the transition to G2, this focus typically shifts, with the siblings taking more of a family-first approach.

## PREDICTABLE PARADOXES: SIBLING PARTNERSHIP STAGE

The Sibling Partnership Stage is the second stage in the family business generation model. Before exploring common Sibling Stage paradoxes, it is helpful to note the typical dynamics of this stage. The stage's greatest challenge involves determining leadership and decision-making approaches. These are made more complex by the naturally high value placed on sibling equality – most sisters and brothers quickly become uncomfortable when one sibling attempts to exert power, with "You're not the boss of me!" a common and heartfelt reaction. Yet, if no sibling is the boss of any other, how can decisions be made? How will direction be set?

The dynamics of the Sibling Partnership Stage are often in stark contrast to those of the Founding Stage, where one powerful and visionary leader is clearly in charge. As in the Founding Stage, a predictable set of paradoxes emerge in the G2 stage (see Figure 3.3). Additionally, the preferences of the founder – for control over trust, action over planning, expediency over patience, proprietorship over stewardship, and roots over wings – also create a predictable set of strengths and weaknesses in the family and business that the siblings will have to address.

### The Sample Transportation siblings

Upon completing high school, the two eldest Sample siblings, George Jr. and Geri, came to work at the business, attending college at night, as their father had. Suzanne and George were surprised when their third child, Suzi, expressed an interest in leaving home to attend college in Denver. But they agreed to her request. Louis, the "baby" of the family, fell in love with the jazz trumpet after hearing some of his mother's old Duke Ellington records, and followed Suzi to Denver immediately after high school, to pursue music. Initially, Louis caught quite a bit of flak from his parents for this move; but George Jr.'s and Geri's presence at the office and general obedience ultimately provided cover for the younger two.

For the Sample family, the transition to the Sibling Partnership Stage hit suddenly and hard. George Sr., who had always put his business's health over his own, experienced an unexpected, severe heart attack at age 50. Although George Jr. was only 27 years old at the time, he had been working full-time at the business for almost ten years. Junior, as he was known, felt ready, willing, and able to take over his father's role. He had been functioning as an assistant to his father, and in that capacity had joined George for every major event or meeting. Although he had never run a department himself, Junior knew all areas of the business, and everyone knew him.

Geri had also been at the business for almost ten years by that time. She had taken full responsibility for several departments, supervising large numbers of people and handling skillfully the ups and downs of customer service and administrative management. Her colleagues had tremendous respect for her. Geri's and Junior's ability to step in for George was a great source of comfort for Suzanne, their mother.

## Sibling Partnership Stage: business paradoxes

As Junior and Geri took the reins at Sample Transportation, they faced one overarching issue: whether and how they would deviate from the path their father had forged. Initially, the two siblings tried to do everything "just like Dad." For example, Junior moved into George Sr.'s office and approached decisions in the controlling, quick, unstructured manner his father had perfected. Also like his father, Junior pursued expansion opportunities aggressively, taking risks that he knew his father would have welcomed.

As the two siblings assumed leadership, they got a closer look at the various businesses that made up Sample Transportation. It was revealing: several of their many businesses had serious profitability and performance problems. George Sr.'s resistance to computers and systems and procedures had led, over the years, to significant disorganization. As such, Junior and Geri felt pressured to turn things around quickly. They continued to make decisions with minimal consultation with others, gathering little information to support their actions. For example, they plunged into buying new technology that ultimately exacerbated several issues. Largely because the Sample siblings embraced a management approach like their father's – emphasizing quick action, control, and expedience – within one year of their taking over, every division of the business was struggling.

Faced with this decline, the siblings decided to take a very different approach – the direct opposite of what their father would have done. Specifically, they forced themselves to place more trust in others. They began to "empower" non-family employees to make decisions independently. For example, they granted control over all computer-system decisions to the non-family supervisor of the repair shop. "You're the expert on your business," they told him. "Do what you think makes sense. We won't get in your way."

Unfortunately, this new hands-off approach also failed. No one in the organization was accustomed to a decentralized, "empowerment" approach, and partly as a result of this, employees lacked the skills or experience to make the decisions they had been assigned. Evidence was everywhere: meetings to decide on computer equipment were interminable; endless hours went toward project planning and data collection; the auto shop still lacked crucial computer systems and controls; no one had clear accountability for a given project, so no one took responsibility for failures.

Finally, after nine wholly unproductive months, the siblings realized they had to find a way to preserve the company's traditional strengths while supplementing them with new, improved approaches. They had to do **both**. They started by reflecting on the difficulties they had faced as new family business leaders. First, they had tried to run things exactly like their father, because his approach had helped him build the business quickly. The siblings' strategy emphasized, exaggerated, and enlarged the weaknesses (such as disorganization) inherent in George's original approach, jeopardizing the business's continued success.

In reaction, the siblings had tried the opposite approach. Where Dad was controlling, they would be trusting. Where Dad moved quickly and instinctively without a clear data-based plan, they would be deliberate and patient. Unfortunately, this swing had led to indecision, pointless data collection, and useless planning and analysis.

Finally, the siblings formulated an approach emphasizing both. They started with a simple strategic plan that would identify the three or four key areas of greatest opportunity for improvement. They involved a select group of strong non-family leaders in the process. The resulting strategy unified the leadership team and set clear direction for it, with delineated roles, responsibilities, and decision-making processes and accountability. The strategic plan embodied the paradox of core *and* opportunistic, leading to two key questions: To what extent would Sample Transportation focus its attention on well-established, highly planned areas that were "core" to the company's identity and expertise? Conversely, to what extent would the company pursue areas that were more "opportunistic" (in other words, less established, less planned, and more diversified)? The group determined that such opportunities were best pursued only after the core was strengthened. Specifically, the business needed to become more professional through more consistent use of systems and processes.

The strategic planning process demonstrated several common paradox-related issues in the Sibling Partnership Stage. First, it showed the preference in that stage for a focus on core business elements, as opposed to the Founding Stage preference for opportunistic business elements. The group's emphasis on systems and procedures showed their preference for process, versus the strong Founding Stage preference for task. Finally, the siblings' decision to delegate more to non-family executives demonstrated the Sibling Partnership Stage preference for collective over individual approaches.

As a final example of paradox in this stage, the sister and brother elected to run the business as a team, acting as "co-CEOs" rather than determining which one merited the top position. In this case, the siblings had complementary skills: employees appreciated Geri's hands-on experience and skill managing large groups of people, along with Junior's exposure to all aspects of the business and its customers. The overall approach of serving as co-leaders reflects a typical Sibling Partnership Stage bias toward equality over merit.

## Sibling Partnership Stage: family paradoxes

Junior and Geri differed significantly from their parents with regard to how they balanced work *and* home, and set family priorities. Both siblings set specific limits on their time at work. Junior ate breakfast with his children almost every morning and coached their soccer and basketball teams. Geri had no children, but participated actively in her church and community, and enjoyed ocean cruises annually. Their father's absence during their own childhoods was a significant motivator of the siblings' focus on work–life balance. In fact, when faced with the paradox of work *and* home, they chose home over work, especially once they had established a more professional management group to run the business in their absence.

George's health never recovered to a point that allowed him to return to the business, although he continued to receive full salary and benefits. Over time, George became comfortable leaving leadership of the business to his two older children. However, he and Suzanne still had important decisions to make, especially regarding ownership of the business among the four siblings. In this decision making, they faced the paradox of merit *and* equality.

Recall that Suzi and Louis, the two younger siblings, lived in Denver, about 60 miles away from their home town. They had never been involved in Sample Transportation and were happy to leave management of the business to Junior and Geri. However, as the years went on and the business prospered, the lifestyles of the two pairs of siblings diverged considerably. Suzi's and Louis' career choices (as a teacher and musician, respectively) brought them modest incomes. Meanwhile, Junior and Geri enjoyed ever-increasing business success, living in large homes, driving upscale company cars, and attending industry meetings in exotic locations multiple times a year. Not surprisingly, at family gatherings for holidays and birthdays, tensions began to rise. Louis and Suzi asked their parents and siblings some tough questions: Would they ever enjoy any financial benefits from the business? Did they have to work in the business to get anything out of it? Would they even be considered for jobs in the business in the first place?

In response, Geri and Junior made clear that they were willing to give their younger siblings a chance to work in the business. After much deliberation, neither Suzi nor Louis opted to move back home. They realized that their talents and interests lay in other domains, and that neither the business career track nor the small town setting was a good fit. Nonetheless, the discussion of sibling employment opened up a frank discussion of sibling ownership. Although they had a simple will, George and Suzanne hadn't faced the full range of their estate-planning decisions. George's focus in the Founding Stage had been on running and growing the business (proprietorship), rather than on passing it to future generations (stewardship). At the urgings of their children, the couple completed their estate planning. Suzanne convinced George to leave ownership of the business equally to all four siblings – 25 percent each. This fitted their parenting philosophy, which had generally emphasized equality, rather than merit, when making decisions regarding their children.

## Sibling Partnership Stage: summary

The two oldest Sample siblings showed tremendous dedication, skill, and teamwork in taking over leadership of the business after their father's unplanned exit. As the years went on, paradoxes typical of the

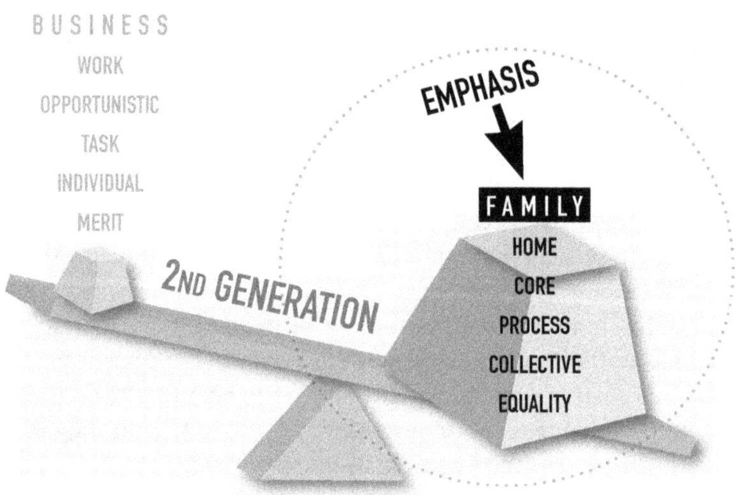


**Figure 3.3** *Sibling Partnership Stage fundamental paradoxes*

Sibling Partnership Stage emerged to challenge them. See Figure 3.3 for a summary. Overall, against their father's preference for a business-first approach, the siblings often put family first. Strategically, they focused on core rather than opportunistic approaches. Their management approach favored process over task. In decision making, they tended to favor collective over individual approaches. In the ownership (and management) of the business, they pursued equality over merit. In terms of their families, they favored home over work. Again, in each of these paradoxes, both sides hold merit. However, the siblings will tend to prefer one side over the other, many times choosing the opposite of what their parents chose in the Founding Stage.

## PREDICTABLE PARADOXES: COUSIN COLLABORATION STAGE

A genogram, or family tree, is a very useful tool for understanding family composition and dynamics across generations. Each sibling in the family, along with their spouse and children, makes up an individual family "branch," as depicted in Figure 3.4 for the Sample family. The genogram also provides a clear visual contrast between the Sibling Partnership and Cousin Collaboration stages.

As the genogram suggests, the Sibling Partnership (G2) is typically smaller and simpler than the Cousin Collaboration (G3). Consequently,

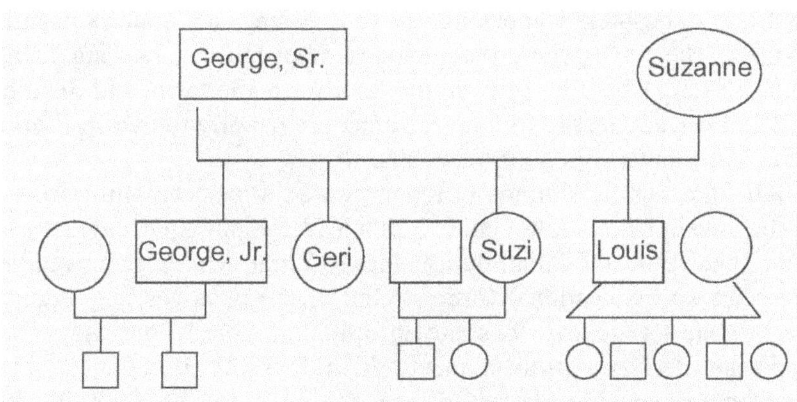


**Figure 3.4** *Sample family tree*

sibling relationships tend to be less complicated but more intense, as the small group size – four siblings in G2 versus nine cousins in G3 – magnifies interpersonal dynamics. This feature, coupled with the natural rivalry among most siblings, results in significant cooperation-related challenges in the Sibling Partnership Stage – siblings know how to push each other's buttons, because they installed them!

In contrast, the Cousin Collaboration Stage usually involves a considerably larger group, presenting a very different set of challenges. For example, a typical cousin group will likely contain a larger variety of viewpoints and approaches than most sibling groups. However, the larger cousin group tends to be less intense than the smaller sibling group, with its sheer numbers diffusing and reducing the emotional intensity of relationships. And, if the cousin group learns to honor its diversity and harness its complexity, it can become a wonderful force to be reckoned with.

Many struggles of the sibling-to-cousin transition are the same no matter the business's industry or location. The family members will face several common paradoxes, as illustrated by a continuation of the Sample family case study.

## Sample Transportation prepares for the cousins

Fast forward 15 years. The family has grown, they have professionalized the business, and the business has prospered. Geri and Junior continue as business leaders and the four siblings continue as business owners. The next generation includes nine cousins, ranging in age from 2 to 22. About half live in the family's home town, and the other half in Denver. George Sr. and Suzanne are happily retired in Florida, completely independent of the business.

All four Sample siblings were committed to a successful transition to the cousin generation. Under Geri's leadership, they decided to join their local university Family Business Center, where they attended meetings and educational forums. One of the practices they adopted was to meet regularly to share information. Rarely did they make important decisions in these meetings. In fact, the siblings had yet to vote on any specific matter. Instead, the meetings largely comprised updates from the two older siblings about significant business developments. The younger siblings complied with the recommendations of their elders, seldom challenging or questioning them.

But the sibling-meeting dynamic changed as several G3 cousins reached age 18. At that point, Junior's two sons joined the business as interns; both showed promise. In contrast, Suzi's and Louis's children had little exposure to or involvement in the business, partly because they lived farther away. In this context, the two younger siblings began to discuss their concerns for their children. They acknowledged to each other that until that point they had contentedly accepted their positions as supportive "outsiders." However, as they saw the same dynamic emerging for their children, they became concerned. So the next time the siblings got together, Suzi and Louis had a raft of questions and concerns for their older siblings, and most of these revolved around predictable paradoxes in the Cousin Collaboration Stage.

## Cousin Collaboration Stage: business paradoxes

Suzi and Louis raised their first set of questions in January, when Junior and Geri gave their customary report on the past year's financial performance. Immediately after the presentation, the younger siblings challenged the practice of reinvesting all profits back into the business. They pointed out that while the older siblings earned generous salaries, neither Louis nor Suzi had gained a cent from their ownership of the business. When would dividends begin? Suzi and Louis had come to terms with their own roles in the business, but they expressed a strong desire for things to be different for their children. Specifically, in the Cousin Collaboration Stage, they wanted to see some opportunities for harvesting some of the value that had been built over the generations, for the benefit of their children, rather than watching the business reinvest all returns back into itself. This is the paradox of harvest *and* invest.

There were other issues. Suzi and Louis expressed frustration with having a lack of information about the business. While they appreciated the regular updates the older siblings provided, they complained that Geri and Junior had maintained a rigid policy of keeping other details of the business, especially financials, completely private. The older siblings argued that keeping key information confidential, especially from their public competitors, was one of their greatest competitive advantages. Given this, they worried that their younger siblings might inadvertently leak information that would erode this advantage. Also, given that the younger siblings were not business savvy, the older siblings worried that they would misunderstand or misinterpret the numbers. As such, Junior and Geri kept the details of their compensation and benefits private, and wished to perpetuate this policy in the third generation. In general, they expressed concern that a large group of cousins could do great damage to the company if they were careless with confidential company information. These issues exemplify the paradox of privacy *and* transparency; the older siblings valued the former, while the younger ones craved more of the latter. Clearly, both privacy *and* transparency have their place, and finding ways to honor both yields the greatest advantages.

The younger siblings brought up yet another issue. Important decisions about the business had always been made by those working inside the business, without any process for involving all four owners. The two older siblings brought information about significant developments to the younger siblings as a courtesy, and their support was viewed as a given. For example, there was never a formal vote regarding major decisions about the business, such as the building of a new corporate headquarters facility or the selling of an unprofitable division. The elder siblings simply presumed that their younger siblings had no strong opinions about such matters, and would consistently support their decisions. In the past, that approach had worked well. But as the family prepared for a larger group of cousins sharing ownership, the younger siblings felt that a more formal approach to decisions would be beneficial. Meanwhile, the insiders saw no need to replace the process of informal consensus they had used to that point. This issue illustrates the paradox of formal *and* informal.

Another issue related to the growing ownership group was emerging. Those in the business felt that owners should speak with one voice at all times, and that owners should rise above their differences. In fact, they preferred an ownership model that concentrated the voting power within those who led the business. Junior and Geri were well aware that a group of owners holding multiple, distinct interests could deeply complicate the running of the business. Thus the older siblings tended to emphasize the power of agreement, as led by them, within the entire extended family. Suzi and Louis, in contrast, had a healthy respect for the diverse needs of branch families: they sought opportunities to accommodate each family's divergent priorities. They also felt that had been quite accommodating of their siblings for the sake of unity for many years, and wished to avoid having their children assume a similar stance. This is the paradox of one family *and* family branch.

## Cousin Collaboration Stage: family paradoxes

Similarly, in the family there were differences related to "insider" and "outsider" status. For example, Suzi and Louis had always been proponents of individual freedom. They had left their small home town and made their lives in the "big city." Neither had regrets about this choice, even though it had distanced each from the broader family. In contrast, Junior and Geri valued loyalty. Unlike their younger siblings, they had stayed home, making sacrifices and compromises in the best interests of the business and, as they saw it, for the family. Thus they were more likely to emphasize the idea of a family with a more unitary focus (primarily on upholding the business). The siblings had accommodated these differences – which are based on the paradox of freedom *and* loyalty – on an ad hoc basis for many years; but as the next generation emerged, each sibling pair felt compelled to defend the benefits of its unique position. For example, each branch worried that the others might impose their values on their children, and felt compelled to protect against this.

## Cousin Collaboration Stage: summary

As the siblings prepared for the transition to the cousin generation, other paradoxes emerged from the "insider-outsider" dynamic. As mentioned earlier, those working in the business wanted to continue investing available resources in the business, while those not working in the business sought to initiate opportunities for disinvesting or harvesting, through distributions or other ownership benefits. In terms of management philosophy, those not working in the business sought more transparency while those working in the business wanted to preserve the current, more privacy-oriented approach. In thinking

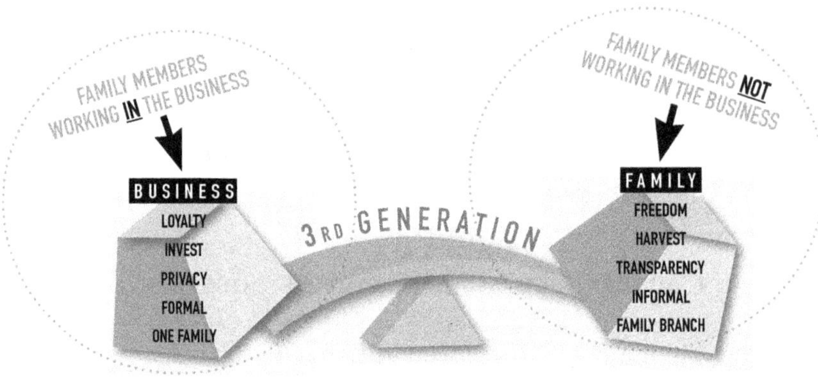


**Figure 3.5** *Cousin Collaboration Stage fundamental paradoxes*

about decision making, the "insiders" leaned towards the established practice of informal, consensus-driven decisions (led by them), where the "outsiders" endorsed more formal, voting-based approaches. See Figure 3.5.

Given these divergences, the dynamics that had been stable and productive for the siblings began to fray as their children became a greater part of the family and business picture. In this context, the concept of paradox provides a useful way of thinking about the differences in perspective between those working in the business and those not working in the business; conflicts between these viewpoints strain the family and business, as Figure 3.5 illustrates. In the big picture, it's important to understand that these groups will tend to have distinct preferences, based on their divergent experiences. Neither perspective is right or wrong: indeed, gaining a full understanding and respect for the other group's point of view can only strengthen the branches' relationships and responses.

## THE ENTERPRISING FAMILY

The Enterprising Family is one that has lived through successive generations of family business management and ownership, dealing effectively with the increasing complexity along the way.[4] Through its generations, the Enterprising Family has felt pressure to choose either a family-first or business-first approach, and has come to recognize that neither approach is correct in and of itself. Both perspectives are needed for continuity. The Enterprising Family has found ways to affirm both family *and* business over time, largely by grappling proactively with many challenging paradoxes over the years. Enterprising Families have the structures in place and the insight needed to support both sides represented in a paradox, and thus have created tremendous business and family vitality across many generations.

The Sample family, for example, has the potential to become an Enterprising Family as the third generation matures and prepares for the fourth generation, of second cousins. If they continue their open dialogue and seek to understand and value all dimensions of the paradoxes they face, they will lay the groundwork for long-term continuity. However, if they become rigid in their preferences and continue to gyrate between business-first and family-first solutions, they will jeopardize their ability to transition smoothly or effectively into the next generation.

Recalling the oscillation model discussed at the beginning of this chapter, the focus of the fourth generation for the Enterprising Family is both, as shown in Figure 3.6. In the fourth stage of the model, the

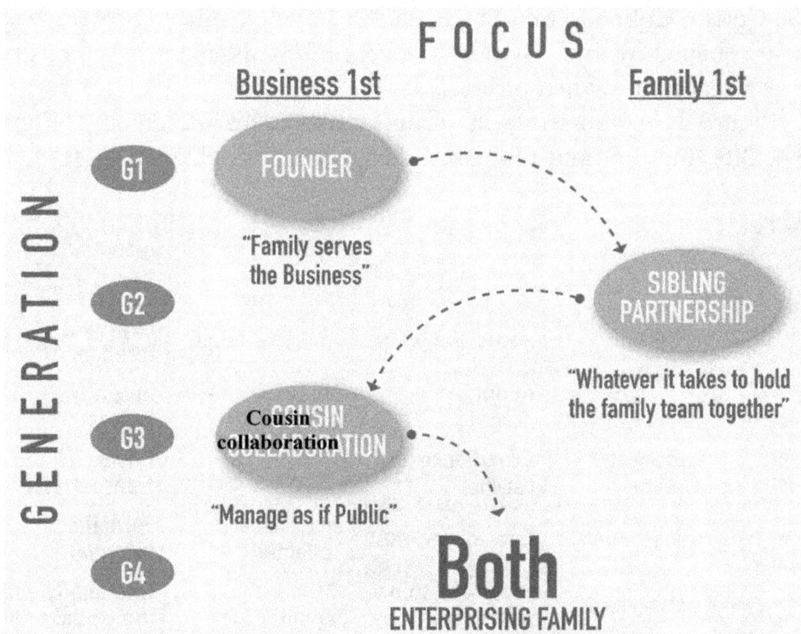


**Figure 3.6** *Generational oscillation and the enterprising family*

Enterprising Family will develop structures and processes that engage and benefit from the active involvement of the entire family – those working in the business and those not working in the business, with all branches pulling together under one vision, that of "One Family."

## GENERATIONAL PARADOXES: FINAL ANALYSIS

The Sample family example provides a great illustration of the paradoxes that accompany each generation of a family business, from Founding to Sibling Partnership to Cousin Collaboration. In the Founding Stage, there is a natural preference for a business-first stance: the founder's dedication to the business and his vision, ingenuity, and hard work usually bring a consistent emphasis on control, expedience, and action. In the Sibling Partnership Stage, the focus oscillates from business first to a compensating family-first stance. Sisters and brothers have to wrestle with the need for both tradition *and* change on their watch, which is often characterized by an emphasis on group processes and equality, and a renewed commitment to home and hearth. Moving into the Cousin Collaboration Stage, we see paradox-related preferences as being shaped by an individual's degree of involvement in the business – as a manager, owner, or both.

Figure 3.7 summarizes the primary paradoxes presented in Figures 3.4, 3.5, and 3.6, and discussed throughout this chapter. Note that in

| Key impact areas | Generations: First | Second | Third |
|---|---|---|---|
| Family priorities | **Roots** *and* wings | Work *and* **home** | **Loyalty** *and* **freedom** |
| Strategic choice | **Action** *and* planning | Opportunistic *and* **core** | **Invest** *and* **harvest** |
| Management philosophy | **Expedience** *and* patience | Task *and* **process** | **Privacy** *and* **transparency** |
| Decision making | **Control** *and* trust | Individual *and* **collective** | **Formal** *and* **informal** |
| Ownership focus | **Proprietorship** *and* stewardship | Merit *and* **equality** | **One family** *and* **individual branch** |

**Figure 3.7** *Summary generational paradoxes*

each generation column, Figure 3.7 places the business-first side of the paradox on the left and the family-first side of the paradox on the right. As discussed, in G1, the Founder shows a strong preference for the business-first side of the paradox (in **bold** in Figure 3.7.) In G2, the siblings show a preference for the family-first side of the paradox (also in **bold** in Figure 3.7.) In G3, the preferred side of the paradox depends on whether the family member is working in the business or not. Those working in the business tend to favor the business-first side of the paradox (the left-hand side in the diagram). Those not working in the business favor the family-first side (the right-hand side in the diagram).

Figure 3.7 also sorts each paradox into a key impact area. In each generation, the primary paradoxes are categorized as relating primarily to family priorities, strategic choice, management philosophy, decision making, or ownership focus.

Although the overview provided in Figure 3.7 is comprehensive, it is not all-inclusive. Many family firms will surely experience paradoxes that are not listed, or will experience one of the listed paradoxes in a way that does not fit neatly into the parameters the figure indicates. This figure, and the Sample family chronology of this chapter, are not meant to be an endpoint. Hopefully, they will serve more as an entry point, an inspiration to explore the paradoxes that have affected your own family's past, present, and future.

In this way, the material presented here can help to demystify the evolution of a family business, especially regarding the generation-based paradoxes encountered. The knowledge gained can support the evolution of a business family into an Enterprising Family.

# 4 Predictable Conflicts in the Intersections

Well-known management consultant Peter Drucker admired Mary Parker Follett as one of the prophets of modern business management.

> As conflict – difference – is here in the world, as we cannot avoid it, we should I think, use it. Instead of condemning it, we should set it to work for us … it is possible to conceive of conflict as not necessarily a wasteful outbreak of incompatibilities but a normal process by which socially valuable differences register themselves for the enrichment of all concerned … conflict as the moment of the appearing and focusing of differences may be a sign of health, a prophecy of progress.[1]
>
> Mary Parker Follett, management thinker and consultant

In the 1920s, Follett explored healthy conflict in organizations as a source of energy needed for change. Her advice is consonant with the practices of many family firms – that it's best to recognize conflict as natural, to capitalize on it, and even to see it as "prophecy of progress." Family businesses certainly know that thoughtfully tackling the conflict inherent in a given problem leads to better understanding and superior results.

## FROM TWO SYSTEMS TO THREE

A fundamentally paradoxical feature of family business is that families tend to be socialistic, while businesses are firmly capitalistic, as introduced in Chapter 1. Family businesses must address this often-conflicting blend of ideologies. To make matters even more complex, likely during the second and third generation, the two systems of family and business evolve into three subsystems: family, management, and ownership. These three subsystems are known as the three-circle model of the family business system as originally introduced by Davis and Tagiuri in 1982.[2] Management and ownership emerge from the business system. This is driven by naturally evolving dynamics in the growing business. For example, some family members begin to see themselves more as owners than managers. Or the management team begins to include more non-family executives in key roles. Or family ownership may be shared more widely. Figure 4.1 depicts this evolution from two subsystems to three.

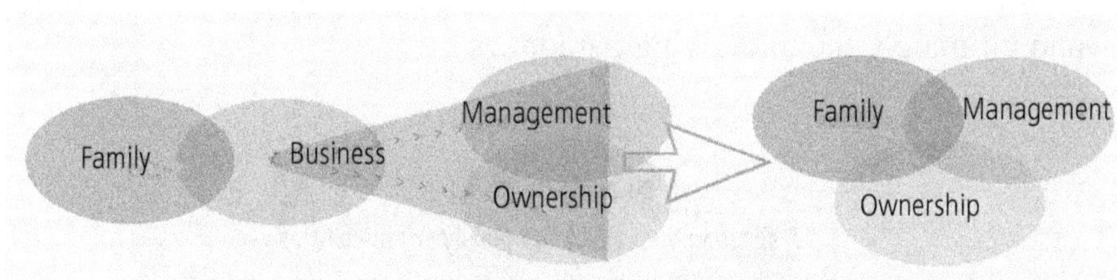


**Figure 4.1** *Family business system evolution*

The three distinct subsystems found in family firms create both problems and opportunities at their intersections – the overlaps among the three circles. Most problems that family businesses face emerge from either these intersections or the generational patterns described in the previous chapter, rather than from individual family members. Appreciating that most problems are common and situation-based, rather than unique and personal, can help families navigate them more successfully. It is also helpful for families to recognize that conflicts created by the system intersections are comprised of contradictions and likely paradoxes.

When problems are identified as paradoxes, established thought processes and techniques can be applied to harness power within the paradoxes, yielding stronger family bonds and a higher-performing business. This approach supports achieving the "health" and "progress" that Follett notes.

A closer examination of the three family business subsystems will be helpful in understanding and addressing the conflicts and contradictions forged within the subsystem intersections. This process will allow the underlying paradox (or paradoxes) to be identified and addressed. Developing appropriate governance structures is an essential component of long-term management of the paradoxes uncovered.

## PROBLEM–CONFLICT–CONTRADICTION–PARADOX

Conflict is often defined as an actual or perceived *opposition* of needs, principles or interests. This definition implies that conflicts include at least one fundamental contradiction, by nature. *If* this contradiction is paradoxical – that is, comprised of two sides that appear to be opposing but are in fact mutually supportive – then there is potential for a *Both/AND* approach. Figure 4.2 presents the process of recognizing the conflict within a problem and, in turn, identifying the contradictions and ultimately the underlying paradoxes.

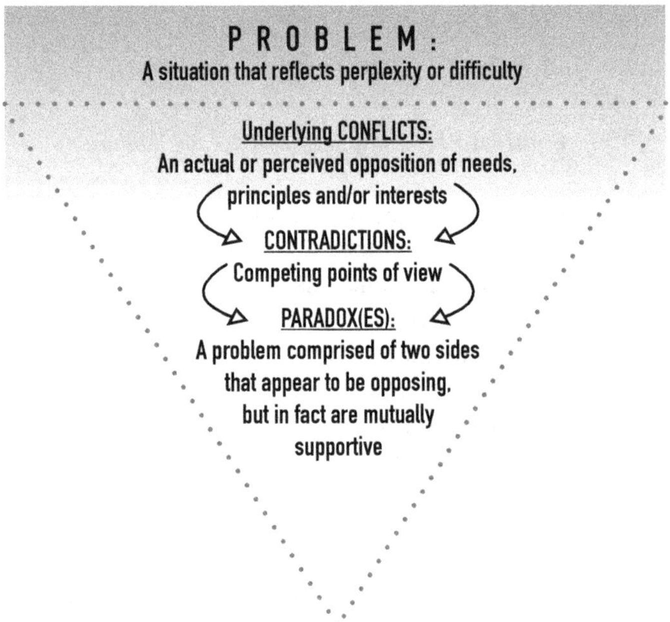


**Figure 4.2** *Problem–conflict–contradiction–paradox process defined*

## UNDERSTANDING THE INTERSECTIONS

Understanding the conflicts and likely contradictions in each intersection is essential. Identifying – and managing – the underlying paradox in the contradiction is key to harnessing the power to bond the family

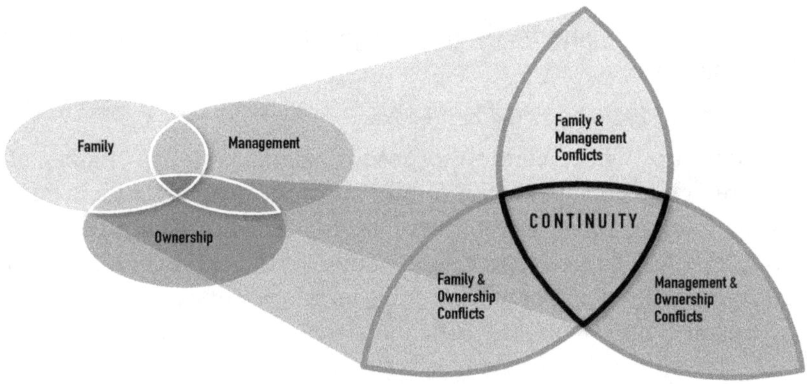


**Figure 4.3** *Intersections in the three subsystems*

and propel the business. Figure 4.3 depicts three areas of potential conflict that emerge at the intersections of family and management, management and ownership, and ownership and family. Subsequent sections of this chapter highlight classic conflicts associated with each intersection.

There are two high-value benefits to addressing the paradoxes that are associated with the contradictions found in the intersections. First, the mutual understanding and support that can be built while managing a given paradox can dissolve much of the personal conflict that stems from the problem area. Second, the family can put effective governance practices into place to anticipate and manage similar problems or other paradox-related conflicts in the future. The family can derive great strength from its capacity to face paradoxes, and the business benefits from the capability to address those paradoxes.

When the family gains an understanding of the central problems and associated paradoxes within each of the three intersections and puts into place the proper governance practices to anticipate and manage these paradoxes, they can enhance greatly their business's *continuity*, which is the overriding objective for most family businesses. In fact, a recent study by the Bank of Korea investigated over 3,000 Japanese firms (all were over 200 years old) and found that the overriding focus of these firms has been continuity, as summarized in the following quote:

their ultimate purpose is not the profit, but its [the company's] continuation.[3]

Continuity is the central purpose of identifying and understanding the predictable and pervasive family business system conflicts that arise in the intersections (as illustrated by Figure 4.3). Using the conflict–contradiction–paradox process to address the ultimate source of the conflict at hand increases the long-term viability and success of the approach taken.

## FAMILY–MANAGEMENT CONFLICTS

This section focuses on some of the more common conflicts that can arise between the points of view of the family and the management in a family business. Figure 4.4 depicts classic conflicts in the family–management intersection.

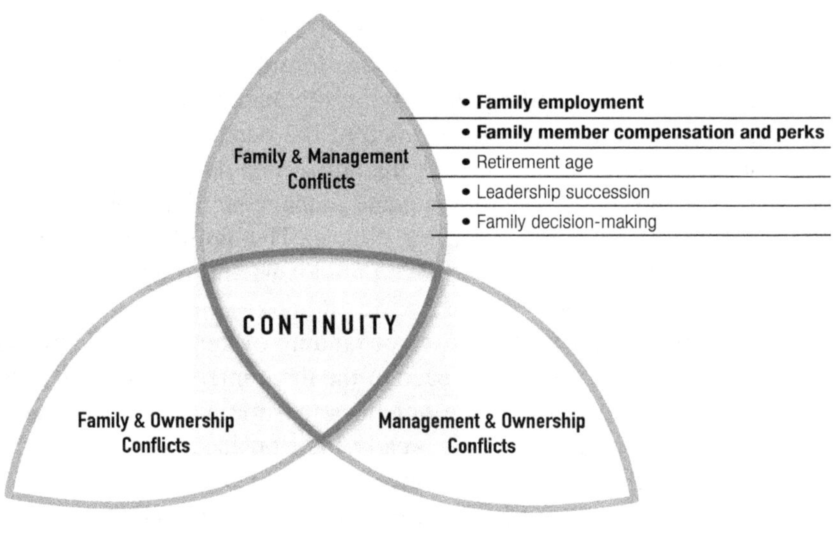


**Figure 4.4** *Family–management conflicts*

Two challenging conflicts at this intersection, family employment and family compensation (**bolded** in the list in Figure 4.4), are presented in Table 4.1, as part of a problem–conflict–contradiction–paradox analysis.

**Table 4.1** *Two examples of family–management conflict*

| Conflict stated as a problem | Classic conflict | Primary contradiction | Underlying paradox |
|---|---|---|---|
| *Which family members can be employed in the family business?* | Family employment | **Side A**: Strict requirements for family members.<br>**Side B**: All family members have a right to be employed. | Selective *and* Inclusive |
| *How to compensate family members?* | Compensation and perks | **Side A**: Based on market.<br>**Side B**: Based on family member need. | Market *and* Need |

Consider the family employment conflict. Within it, one fundamental contradiction is whether employment in the business should require a set of particular requirements (such as specific professional qualifications) or whether it should be an opportunity available to all family members. This isn't necessarily the only contradiction inherent in the family employment conflict; for example, another contradiction might be whether grandchildren should be encouraged to stay in the family's home town or encouraged to see more of the world. In managing problems found in the intersections, it's important to identify the *primary* contradictions. That, of course, requires careful listening and exploration. In this particular case, the primary contradiction is as stated above: strict requirements versus an open-door policy for family employment.

The next step involves considering whether the contradiction has two sides that are both valid. In this case, family employment has two viable, seemingly opposing sides, so we must proceed to identifying the underlying paradox. The paradox of selective *and* inclusive is identified. Like all paradoxes, it contains two sides that *appear* to be in conflict – employment policies that are highly selective, and employment policies that are highly inclusive. There are strong arguments for both sides. Although the two sides, inclusive *and* selective, appear to be in conflict, upon closer examination they are determined to be mutually supportive.

When considering family involvement in the business, there are times to be very welcoming, and times to be more selective. Emphasizing either one of these two sides of the paradox to the exclusion of the other will likely cause immediate problems or new problems over time. Respecting the wisdom found in each side – both inclusive *and* selective – is the way to harness the paradox's full potential.

Also recognize that for a given conflict, there may be associated problems requiring "tough decisions." These problems that need to be solved in the family–management intersection can also be challenging, but they must be faced. It is interesting to note that, once decided, some of these problems – but not all of them – may reveal paradoxes to be managed going forward. Table 4.2 illustrates examples of typical problems requiring decisions in the area of family employment, with possible associated paradoxes.

**Table 4.2** *Example problems to be solved – family employment*

| Problem to be solved | Decision type | Paradox within the problem |
|---|---|---|
| Will we hire in-laws? | Yes or no | Inclusive *and* Selective |
| Do family members need to have outside work experience? | Yes or no | None |
| Will we find a job for our kids so they can stay close to home? | Yes or no | Roots *and* Wings |

The second example of a family–management conflict noted in Table 4.1 is family member compensation, and the associated primary contradiction of market-based pay versus compensation based on family member seniority and need: the paradox of market *and* need emerges from that contradiction. However, as with the employment conflict above, it's possible this conflict has other inherent contradictions, such as issues related to minimizing taxes. If that were the primary contradiction, it might merely represent a specific problem to solve, perhaps by consulting with the business's accounting firm or asking an independent board to finalize tax-related decisions.

If there is a paradox present, it must be managed rather than solved. In line with this, in this example, both sides – market *and* need – contain truth; in the long run, both truths must be pursued. It's important to define the primary contradiction accurately, and then look deeper in order to identify within the contradiction the paradox that needs to be managed.

Family employment-related and family compensation-related problems are inevitable. They do not emerge from individuals; rather, they result from the intersection of the two systems of family and management. Families committed to continuity will work to anticipate these problems and to create a dialogue and process to analyze them carefully. More specifically, they will likely have to create or revise a governance process to support management of the paradoxes uncovered. The best-documented governance vehicles for family–management intersections are *policies* that help to manage different expectations and perspectives.

Policies can also prevent conflicts from happening in the first place. Achieving success in the process of developing the policies will strengthen the family's confidence and competence, and help the business move forward with less distraction. Using policies as a key tool for managing problems in the system intersections supports the principle that the issues are related less to specific individuals and more to systems and structures. Table 4.7 at the end of this chapter presents two sample policies that can help manage the intersection between family and management.

## MANAGEMENT–OWNERSHIP CONFLICTS

This section focuses on conflicts between the points of view of the management and the ownership in a family business. Figure 4.5 depicts some of the classic conflicts at the management–ownership intersection.

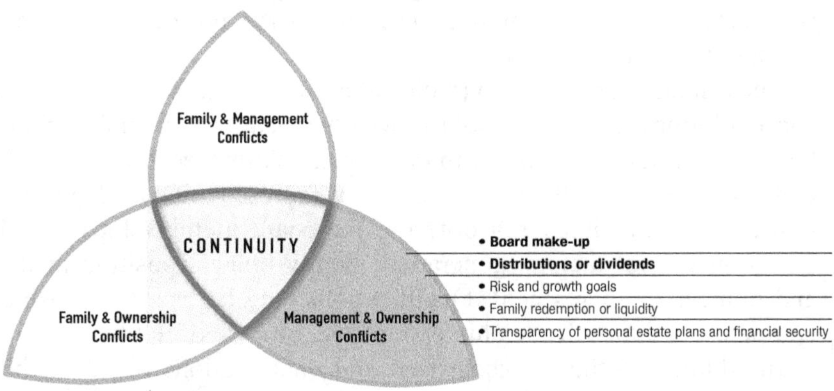


**Figure 4.5** *Management–ownership conflicts*

For this intersection, two specific conflicts related to board make-up and distributions/dividends will be examined in more detail.

**Table 4.3** *Two examples of management–ownership conflict*

| **Conflict stated as a problem** | **Classic conflict** | **Primary contradiction** | Underlying paradox |
|---|---|---|---|
| *Who will serve on the board?* | Board make-up | **Side A**: Based on family relationship<br>**Side B**: Based on skills and experience | Representation *and* Qualifications |
| *How much to pay out in dividend distributions?* | Dividends/ distributions | **Side A**: Distributions for family owners to reward their investment<br>**Side B**: Preserve cash in the business for future investment | Harvest *and* Invest |

Selecting a family business's board of directors is typically a challenging task: management has one set of needs and a specific point of view related to this issue; ownership's needs and point of view can differ significantly. Controlling owners in the family often have the view that participation on the board is a right based on family position. For example, the only son of a business-founding mother may feel "protective" of the family's values or of his children's future involvement in the business, and this would influence his viewpoint on board make-up. Management, on the other hand, may believe that having too many family members on the board detracts from the business, as family board members may bring too few special skills and contacts (for instance, with potential customers) to the business to promote market insight and growth.

The primary contradiction (which a family may arrive at by listening and exploring) in this example is whether board membership should be based on family relationship or business skills (see Table 4.3). The underlying paradox, then, may be that of representation *and* qualifications. Representation (as a criterion for board membership) may be based on several factors: generation, family branch, position in firm, and number of shares held. Qualifications may be based on business competence, family leadership experience, or style of thinking.

In addition to the representation *and* qualifications paradox, there also may be problems that need to be solved related to this conflict regarding who will serve on the board. These problems requiring a decision may house additional paradoxes to be managed. As provided earlier for problems related to family employment, Table 4.4 illustrates some of the problems commonly found in the area of family boards of directors.

**Table 4.4** *Example problems to be solved – board make-up*

| Problem to be solved | Decision type | Paradox within the problem being solved? |
|---|---|---|
| How big a board will be most effective? | Choose | None |
| What proportion of the board will be family owners? | Choose | Merit *and* Representation |
| Will the chair and the CEO be the same person? | Yes or no? | None |

A second common management–ownership conflict is how much to pay out in dividends/distributions. For many, the contradiction is between retaining capital and profits for business growth and security. or paying monies out for the yield and security of the owners (see Table 4.3). Top management typically prefers the former; family members owning a large number of shares and not employed in the business prefer the latter. Framed as such, the underlying paradox is harvest (yield) *and* invest. Harvest can refer to the return of capital to reward the investor, or to prepare the investor for estate-planning liquidity or personal security or philanthropy. Invest refers to deployment of capital towards business growth opportunities.

As with the intersection between family and management, this intersection will benefit from governance that likely includes a set of *rules*, which are usually found in the shareholders' agreement. The rules may address board make-up, dividend approval processes, redemption and valuation formulas, and many other issues, See Table 4.7 at the end of the chapter for examples.

## OWNERSHIP–FAMILY CONFLICTS

This section focuses on conflicts between the points of view of the ownership and the family involved in a family business, as depicted in

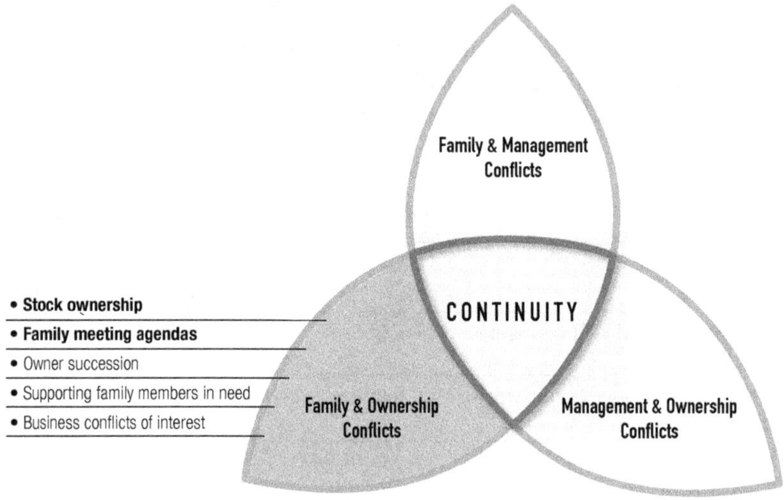


**Figure 4.6** *Ownership–family conflicts*

Figure 4.6. Fundamentally, ownership has two dimensions: economic ownership and emotional ownership. The potential differences in point of view are many. But in the long run, both economics and emotion are essential. If the purpose is only economics, the family's interest in the business and willingness to make sacrifices on its behalf will weaken. If the purpose is solely emotional, the business's competitiveness will almost inevitably wane. Such differences underlie many of the conflicts and paradoxes in this intersection. Some of the classic conflicts at the ownership–family intersection are noted in Figure 4.6.

**Table 4.5** *Two examples of ownership–family conflict*

| Conflict stated as a problem | Classic conflict | Primary contradiction | Underlying paradox |
|---|---|---|---|
| *Who will own stock?* | Rights for ownership | **Side A**: All family members.<br>**Side B**: Based on participation and contribution. | Equality *and* merit |
| *How do we spend our meeting time together?* | Family meetings | **Side A**: Meeting attendance limited and focused on business.<br>**Side B**: Meeting attendance open and focused on relationships. | Work *and* fun |

Two conflicts in this area are examined further: stock ownership and family meeting agendas, as summarized in Table 4.5. The question of who will inherit or receive the family's ownership shares represents an issue that is not only challenging but typically very intense, largely because it contains a contradiction. One argument is for ownership shares to follow family lines, as the parents choose. The other argument is for ownership (and/or power) to be more proportionate to the individual contribution and participation in the business' success. The contradiction here contains a fundamental family–ownership paradox: equality *and* merit.

As with the prior two intersections, the intersection between ownership and family will likely also contain problems needing to be solved, not just paradoxes to be managed. Table 4.6 provides several examples of potential problems to be solved and paradoxes that might be found in the area of stock ownership.

**Table 4.6** *Example problems to be solved – stock ownership*

| Problem to be solved | Decision type | Paradox within the problem being solved? |
|---|---|---|
| Will stock be placed in trusts or owned outright? | Choose | Fixed *and* flexible |
| Can in-laws own stock? | Yes or no | Inclusion *and* exclusion |
| At what age will benefits flow to beneficiaries? | Choose | Control *and* trust |

The second ownership–family conflict to be explored concerns the tone and agenda of family meetings. The contradiction inherent in this issue can be expressed through two questions: If paid for by the business, as is common practice, should the meetings be open only to actual stockholders (for example, with no non-shareholding spouses invited), focused squarely on business issues, and organized to be efficient and frugal? Or should the meetings welcome attendance by all family members, spouses included, and be primarily a time to strengthen family ties and to make the responsibilities of ownership more enjoyable?

Underlying the primary contradiction expressed here is a fundamental paradox of life in general: work *and* play. In the intersection between ownership and family, the paradox could be characterized as work *and* fun. Significant evidence from research on teams and families would suggest that it's ideal to value both.

Given the challenges represented by paradoxes in this area, it's surprising how many business-owning families do not attend more actively to their values, vision, and goals. In contrast, shareholders' rules are much more common, and many contain the types of policies discussed in this chapter. Perhaps that is because these governance vehicles are more explicit, more easily formalized, and more "operational." Yet the owning family's values, vision, and goals often provide the best vehicle for expressing mutually supportive principles and aspirations, and should not be overlooked.

The governance vehicle often used to handle paradoxes in this intersection (including those of merit *and* equality, and work *and* fun) is the owning family's statement of values, vision, and goals. Table 4.7 at the chapter's end presents two examples.

## GOVERNANCE STRUCTURES

The problems–conflicts–contradictions–paradoxes found in each of the three intersections have been explored in some depth so far. This

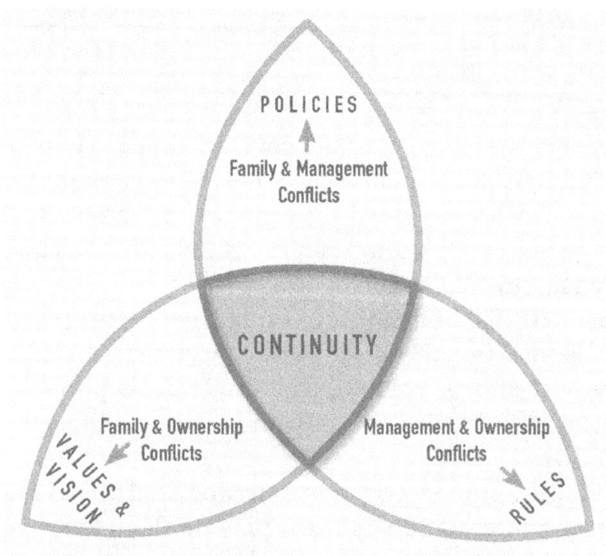


**Figure 4.7** *Governance structures needed*

process focuses on identifying the critical paradoxes to be managed to ensure long-term success. Long-term success can be achieved by developing and implementing specific governance practices, either as a result of a specific conflict encountered or in anticipation of a conflict. The governance practices typically put in place to manage, and in some cases anticipate, conflicts that arise in the intersections of the three family business systems are depicted in Figure 4.7, and are often collected in a family constitution or family charter. Note that each intersection has an associated optimal governance vehicle, and Table 4.7 gives two examples of each vehicle.

**Table 4.7** *Governance vehicles by intersection*

| Intersection | Governance vehicle* | Examples |
|---|---|---|
| Family–Management | Policies | ■ *Family employment policy* – which family members can be employed; conditions of same.<br>■ *Helping family members in need* – how the family intends to support members, both financially and non-financially. |
| Management–Ownership | Rules | ■ *Shareholders agreement* – who can own stock, how it will be valued.<br>■ *Estate plans* – how and when ownership will be transferred. |
| Family–Ownership | Values/vision | ■ *Family values statement* – guiding principles to shape decisions and actions.<br>■ *Family vision statement* – inspiring picture of what family will create together. |

* The authors recommend several resources for more information on governance vehicles related to the family business system intersections discussed in this chapter: for family-management conflicts, *Developing Family Business Policies* by Craig E. Aronoff, Joseph H. Astrachan and John L. Ward (Georgia: Family Enterprises Publishers, 1992); for management-ownership conflicts, *Creating Effective Boards for Private Enterprises: Meeting the Challenges of Continuity and Competition* by John L. Ward (Georgia: Family Enterprises Publishers, 1992); for family-ownership conflicts, *Family Business Ownership: How to be an Effective Shareholder* by Craig E. Aronoff and John L. Ward (Georgia: Family Enterprises Publishers, 1992).

The governance vehicles listed in Table 4.7 are highly effective in managing the paradoxes that arise at the intersections of the three subsystems – family, ownership, and management. In fact, most family businesses have at least one, if not all, of these governance vehicles.

Enterprising Families, who have been successful in achieving continuity across the generations, devote significant resources to developing and managing these governance vehicles. Best practices in family business literature have recommended these approaches for many years. This model, illustrated in Figure 4.7, connects specific conflicts in the three ovals to their related governance best practices.

## INTERSECTIONS: FINAL ANALYSIS

The family–management–ownership system contains three intersections representing potential conflicts among three different pairs of perspectives (see Table 4.8 for a summary of the specific conflicts discussed in this chapter). The conflicts are all the more troublesome because they contain contradictions that reflect real differences in personal perspectives. Therefore, the problems that arise are often attributed to personal differences even though they emerge not from individuals but from the intersections of the subsystems.

The most effective means of handling these problems is to analyze the conflicts associated with them for inherent contradictions, then to dig deeper, in search of the primary underlying paradox, and ultimately to address the paradox with strong governance vehicles (such as policies, rules, or values), including the use of a family constitution. When both sides of the paradox are acknowledged and addressed in this way, conflicts subside and continuity is promoted. In fact, effective governance harnesses the energy of the paradox and often prevents associated problems from arising in the first place.

**Table 4.8** *Family business system intersections summary*

| System intersection | Conflict stated as a problem | Common conflict | Primary contradiction | Underlying paradox | Governance vehicle |
|---|---|---|---|---|---|
| Family–Management | *Which family members can be employed in the family business?* | Family employment | **Position A**: Strict requirements for family members.<br>**Position B**: All family members have a right to be employed. | Selective *and* Inclusive | Policies |
| | *How to compensate family members?* | Compensation and perks | **Position A**: Based on market<br>**Position B**: Based on family member need | Market *and* Need | |
| Management–Owner | *Who will serve on the board?* | Board make-up | **Position A**: Based on family relationship.<br>**Position B**: Based on skills and experience. | Representation *and* Qualifications | Rules (e.g., stockholder agreement) |
| | *How much to pay out in dividends and/or distributions?* | Dividends/ distributions | **Position A**: Distribute to family owners to reward their investment.<br>**Position B**: Preserve cash in the business for future investment. | Harvest *and* Invest | |
| Family–Owner | *Who will own shares?* | Rights for ownership | **Position A**: All family members.<br>**Position B**: Based on participation and contribution. | Equality *and* Merit | Owners' values/ vision/goals |
| | *How do we spend our meeting time together?* | Family meetings | **Position A**: Meeting attendance limited and focused on business.<br>**Position B**: Meeting attendance open and focused on relationships. | Work *and* Fun | |

*This page intentionally left blank*

# Part III

# Managing **Both**

If we choose to live a more spiritual life then we need to become more spontaneous, more engaged and more contemplative.
Living a spiritual life means we are able to live our life in total polarity.
This means we are at ease in the in between spaces:

– between tradition and progressive viewpoints
– between rational and emotional responses
– between taking action and just being there
– between solitude and leisure
– between fasting and feast
– between discipline and wildness.

If we are not growing in our spiritual life then we get stuck on one end of the spectrum or other and we can end up bland, lukewarm, mediocre and isolated. The only way to live a spiritual life is to be able to touch both sides at the same time. Knowing that it is in the interplay between living the spectrum (of these opposite polar forces) that we deepen our spirituality and become more aware of who we are, whom we choose to be and in challenging times how we show up.[1]

Saint Teresa of Avila, 1515

# 5 A Continuum for Addressing Paradoxes

Paradoxes have intrigued great thinkers throughout history and led to wonderful and useful insights:

> I would not give a fig for the simplicity this side of complexity but I would give my life for the simplicity on the other side of complexity.[1]
>
> Oliver Wendell Holmes

In his book *The Executive's Compass: Business and the Good Society,* James O'Toole elaborates on Holmes's wisdom:

> To move beyond the confusion of complexity, executives must abandon their constant search for the immediately practical and, paradoxically, seek to understand the underlying ideas and values that have shaped the world they work in. Managers who clamor for how-to instruction are, by definition, stuck on the near side of complexity.[2]

As discussed earlier and touched on by the opening quote to this chapter, there are two general methods to addressing problems. Algorithmic or "how to" problem solving seeks simplicity. Heuristic thinking or "understanding the underlying values" seeks simplicity on the other side of complexity. Both algorithmic *and* heuristic approaches are necessary to manage paradoxes effectively.

The "Plan, Do, Check, Act" problem-solving process promoted in the field of total quality management provides an example of more algorithmic problem solving. The method is typically carried out as follows:

1 Understand the problem, assess the alternatives, and decide on an action (Plan).
2 Implement the chosen action (Do).
3 Review the outcome to confirm the problem was solved (Check).
4 Take corrective action as needed (Act).

This problem-solving process, like many other algorithmic approaches, focuses on finding a solution, or reaching an endpoint, and has proven very effective over many decades of use. The point of this book is not to dismiss more traditionally algorithmic methods. Indeed, algorithmic methods will be presented as part of the approach to paradox management. However, these popular, more algorithmic methods can be incomplete, especially when addressing paradoxical problems. In such cases, additional emphasis on using both algorithmic *and* heuristic approaches is necessary.

## EITHER/OR – BOTH/*AND*

There are a variety of approaches to addressing paradoxes, representing a range of effectiveness. Figure 5.1 presents these approaches as points on a continuum. Although six separate and distinct approaches are identified, in many cases there is considerable overlap among them. The three traditionally more algorithmic approaches are labeled "Either/Or," and are likely more familiar. They are most effective for less conflictual problems and/or tasks needing a decision or solution.

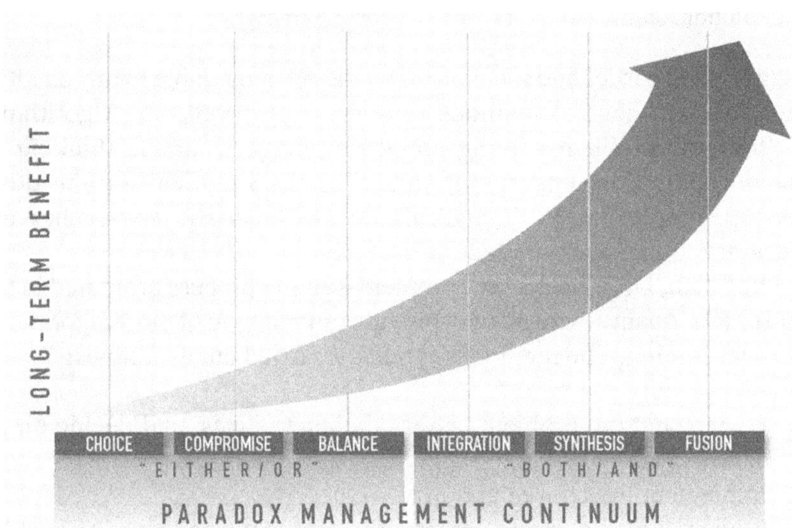


**Figure 5.1** *Paradox management continuum*

But if matters are conflictual, intense, and emotional (as they likely would be for family members), it will be worth the effort to adopt one of the approaches on the right side of the continuum. These three approaches have more heuristics involved and are labeled "Both/*AND*." A Both/*AND* approach provides more significant long-term benefits, as it captures the energy inherent in the two seemingly opposing sides of a paradox. When successful, Both/*AND* methods have the power to strengthen family bonds. Both/*AND* respects both perspectives and offers opportunities for new learning and better insights by addressing both sides of the paradox.

## THE PARADOX MANAGEMENT CONTINUUM

Figure 5.1 illustrates six approaches to paradoxical problems. As shown, the approaches from left to right offer increasingly greater long-term benefits. The remainder of this chapter explains the approaches and applies them to three classic conflicts involving subsystem intersections as identified in the previous chapter.

### Either/Or approaches

In the domain of Either/Or, there are three approaches to explore. The first, Choice, involves simply picking one side of the paradox over the other. The second, Compromise, seeks to minimize the weaknesses present in either side of the paradox. Finally, Balance is about working to exploit some of the opportunities each side of the paradox represents. Implicit, then, within Either/Or, is a decision to minimize weaknesses or to exploit opportunities. This should seem familiar: it is much akin to creating a list of pros and cons and then promoting the option with more advantages or accepting the lesser of the evils uncovered. In problem-solving scenarios where making a yes/no decision is required, Either/Or works well; however, it is a less optimal approach for handling paradoxes.

In general, the goal when approaching paradoxical problems is to push to the far right end of the continuum and use Both/*AND* approaches. This allows the family and the business to gain greater long-term benefits for their efforts. That said, there are times when pushing to Both/*AND* is beyond what the organization, management, or other stakeholders are able to handle. In these cases, it may make good sense to approach the paradox with an Either/Or approach. However, paradoxes addressed in this manner will likely return in the form of the same or a related problem in the future. At that point, a different approach may be warranted. Alternatively, the family business could proactively monitor the initial Either/Or solution, with the idea of implementing a Both/*AND* approach once the organization is in a better position to do so.

## Both/*AND* approaches

Both/*AND* also consists of three approaches along the continuum. The first, Integration, involves identifying the paradox and then maximizing the opportunities present on each side while minimizing the weaknesses. The next chapter will introduce a Polarity Map™ to assist in reaching Integration. Synthesis, the second Both/*AND* approach, seeks to achieve both sides of the paradox simultaneously, yielding greater long-term benefits. Finally, Fusion represents a fundamental shift in thinking about the paradox. This approach aims to create proactive, systemic, and sustainable processes to address the sources and precursors of the problem, preventing it from becoming a problem in the first place. Table 5.1 summarizes the six approaches along the continuum.

**Table 5.1** *Paradox management continuum defined*

| Type | Continuum | Definition |
|---|---|---|
| Either/Or | Choice | Select one of two contradictory alternatives. |
| | Compromise | Minimize the weaknesses of each alternative. |
| | Balance | Maximize the opportunities of each alternative. |
| Both/*AND* | Integration | Identify the problem as a paradox; maximize the opportunities *and* minimize the weaknesses of **both** sides. |
| | Synthesis | Achieve **both** sides of the paradox simultaneously. |
| | Fusion | Anticipate a problem as a paradox and implement a systemic approach that achieves **both** sides. |

Although they are presented as separate and distinct, there can be overlap, especially between adjacent approaches.

Inherent in each approach along the paradox management continuum are trade-offs. Overall, the first three approaches on the continuum offer less in the way of long-term benefits, as they address the paradox in a more limited way. That's not to say that an Either/Or approach is *never* optimal; it may well be the best approach in certain circumstances, as suggested earlier. Nonetheless, it is important, whenever possible, to push past the potential simplicity of an Either/Or approach and through the complexity to reach the Both/*AND* side of the continuum.

## FAMILY EMPLOYMENT ON THE CONTINUUM

To understand application of the paradox management continuum further, return to one of the classic family business conflicts discussed in Chapter 4, family employment. As discussed there, the first step in approaching a problem of this sort is to define exactly what the problem is. The underlying problem will typically be stated along these lines: "How do we address family members who want to participate in the family business?" The responses will likely fall into one of two categories: the business-oriented view ("To work here, first you must work elsewhere, get a degree and develop some qualifications") and the family-oriented view ("All in the family are welcome as employees").

For the sake of this example, here is how the contradiction might be articulated:

**Side A**: Before you can enter the family business you must have three to five years of full-time, outside experience and an advanced university degree.
**Side B**: No specific qualifications. All family members welcome.

### Either/Or approaches: Family employment

This section presents details on each Either/Or approach as applied to the issue of family employment.

### *Choice*

Choice is the first Either/Or approach on the continuum. In this approach, someone within the family business, likely the president or CEO, decides whether or not a family member will be employed. The CEO's choice is based upon his or her specific point of view regarding the family business and its priorities (as might be identified with the Family First–Business First Assessment presented in Part I on p. 18). If the CEO has more of a business-first focus, the policy may require family members to apply for open positions; then the existing performance management system will weed out those with less ability to contribute. On the other hand, if the CEO's focus is more family-first, then it is more likely that the business will provide a position for all interested family members.

The real disadvantage to the Choice approach is that the family members holding views opposing the policy implemented will feel that they have "lost." And the business may well lose too, because depending on the policy chosen, some family members who could make strong contributions might not be able to do so; or in other circumstances, the entry of unqualified family members into the business will diminish overall performance. Choice is more of a short-term approach.

### *Compromise*

The next approach on the continuum is Compromise. Here, the focus is on trying to reduce the weaknesses of each side of the paradox. In the case of family employment, one side wants applicants to have substantial years of experience plus an advanced degree, while the other side wants no specific requirements. As the name of the Compromise approach suggests, one solution is to split the difference. Thus the employment policy might state that interested individuals must have at least two years of outside experience (rather than none, or three to five years) and must attend at least a three-month executive education course (rather than holding no degree or an advanced one) before joining the business. The disadvantage to this approach is that neither side really gets what it wants. By definition, a compromise is the settlement of a dispute such that each side accepts less than what it originally wanted. Thus Compromise, too, is more focused on short-term resolution.

### *Balance*

Balance is the third approach on the continuum. It seeks to maximize the opportunities of each alternative. One example of a Balanced approach to family employment is to employ no more than one member of each couple or from each family branch, so as not to overload the business with family members. By encouraging representative family members to work in the business without overburdening the business, this approach gives each side some of what it desires.

At the same time, it falls short of achieving superior long-term benefit for the family business, because limiting the number of family employees does not necessarily ensure that the most qualified members will enter the business. It's important to seek an approach that serves both sides of the issue: interest in participation and business competence. That means moving further to the continuum's right side: Both/*AND*.

## Both/***AND*** approaches

A Both/*AND* approach is based on the recognition that a paradox contains two sides, that both have merit and must both be seized. Moving to the right side of the continuum allows the family and its business to achieve longer-term results (as suggested by the graph presented in Figure 5.1, repeated here).

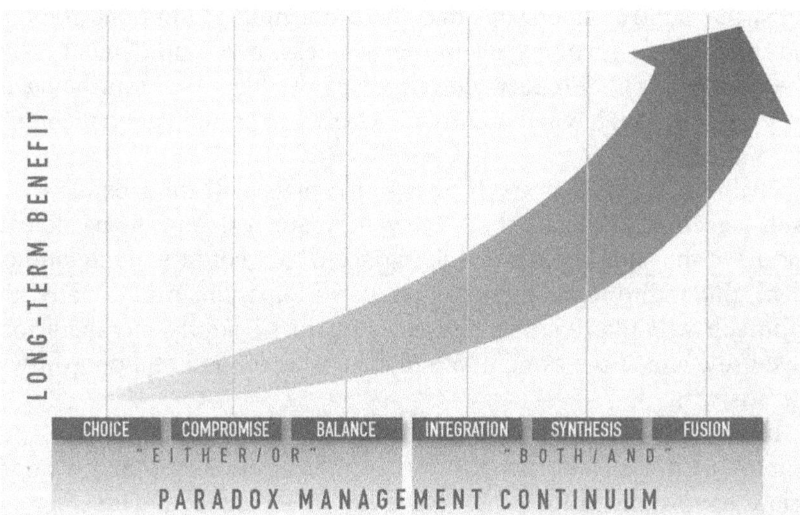

### *Integration*

Beginning with the Integration approach, the first step is to identify the paradox underlying the conflicting points of view. For the family employment case, as previously discussed, the paradox is selective *and* inclusive.

Upon recognizing the paradox as that of selective *and* inclusive, the family can begin to identify the opportunities and weaknesses of each side of the paradox, as a step toward developing an Integration approach. While the Compromise approach focused on minimizing the weaknesses of each side and the Balance option focused on promoting the benefits, Integration takes more of a comprehensive approach to the paradox by focusing on the opportunities *and* weaknesses of both sides. (The next chapter will provide a tool, the Polarity Map™, which aids in developing effective Integration approaches to classic family business paradoxes. Specifically, the Polarity Map™ helps a family business to reach consensus on the opportunities and weaknesses of each side of the paradox.)

For family employment challenges, Integration of the paradox of selective *and* inclusive is accomplished by finding a way to promote both the desires of each family member *and* the needs of the business-owning family as a whole. One way to do this is by reframing the problem as one related to *family involvement* in general, as opposed to the more narrow issue of company employment. Taking this view helps the family understand that there are multiple options for individuals seeking involvement in the business, and employment is just one of these. This broader view releases the business from being the only outlet through which family members can participate in the family and its business.

In this context, it is likely that individuals will do a better job of "self-selection" because they know they are welcome to participate, and have multiple options for doing so, which could include employment, philanthropy, or family council participation. Additionally, this approach will likely attract the most qualified family members for a given role and at the same time reduce the likelihood of a poor fit with the business.

In sum, an Integration approach succeeds by reframing the employment issue as one of involvement, and maximizing appropriate opportunities for both selectivity *and* inclusion. This approach recognizes that some roles (such as management) will require more selectivity and careful matching between role responsibilities and qualifications, while others (such as philanthropy-related roles) lend themselves to more inclusivity, as they require fewer or different formal qualifications.

### *Synthesis*

The next Both/AND paradox management approach is Synthesis. In using this approach, family members will move beyond identifying and addressing both sides of the paradox to reach a point where they no longer see the two sides as opposing and separate. Synthesis is achieved when the classic conflict in question is expressed as a complementary relationship – in this case, when selectivity is inclusive and inclusivity is selective. This is the elegance of Synthesis. Consider the following example of how one family used Synthesis to address family involvement.

Rather than following a fixed set of rules focused on selectivity, family members were asked to conduct their own research into the pros and cons of selective and inclusive approaches to family involvement. They were asked to identify and interview at least two people *inside* the family who held differing points of view about selectivity and inclusivity, and at least two people *outside* the family holding each point of view.

As a next step, family members were asked to summarize their learning and create a personal action plan to address the weaknesses of the choice they preferred. For example, if they choose to join without significant outside work experience, they might propose to address that lack of outside perspective and accountability by taking a part-time leadership role in a community non-profit organization, or in an industry association. They might also propose to have a career coach to review – and enhance – their performance at the business and elsewhere. A task force of the family and the independent directors on the business' board might coach the member through research and action plan development.

As a result, the business benefits from the involvement of thoughtful, disciplined family members willing to prove their commitment to the company and the family, and the family members are served by making the effort to understand the options available to them, how they might benefit (or not) from these, and how the business might benefit (or not). With this Synthesis approach, the interested family member gains additional benefits of self-discovery, insight, and learning, as well as personal responsibility. The family as a whole also has the opportunity to learn from individual family members' research.

### *Fusion*

Fusion, on the far right of the continuum, is the sixth paradox management approach. It involves implementing a systematic process for preventing the emergence of a significant problem or conflict. Fusion leads to the best of both truths of the paradox being realized much more organically. If it's a classic family business contradiction, the interests of both the family *and* the business are served in an optimal manner. This is naturally a challenging goal, and not always attainable. But here's how one family achieved Fusion for family involvement.

In this family, after decades of trial and error-rich experience, the fourth-generation family members developed a career coaching and personnel development process sponsored by the family council. From an early age, younger members of the family hear of and witness the adults taking advantage of these resources to identify their strengths and weaknesses, and to learn what skills and expectations every role in the family's enterprises involves. Family members are accustomed to seeing other family members participate in development and performance assessments for any role they aspire to.

Each young adult also has a personal champion from among the family, and, at the appropriate age, a personal coach. They know they are welcome to participate in any internship or learning opportunity (inside or outside of the business) they wish. As a result, each member feels grateful for the deep interest the family takes in their development and the personal support they receive for it. Each also knows that roles in the family business are best filled by the individuals most committed to them and qualified for them. The family works to identify new opportunities for involvement, and continuously reviews and revises its process for helping members take advantage of these. Not surprisingly, the Fusion the family has achieved with regard to family development has helped promote increases on its confidential "family member satisfaction" survey for three consecutive years.

## THE ART OF PARADOX MANAGEMENT

The six approaches on the paradox management continuum provide a range of options for addressing paradoxes as they emerge. Paradox management is both science *and* art. Some paradoxes are best simplified and addressed more algorithmically, through Either/Or approaches. Others call for greater and more patient efforts, as the stakes are higher. The more heuristic or Both/*AND* approaches offer greater benefits, but at the same time carry more ambiguity and uncertainty, especially in the short run; herein lies the art.

The authors have had success applying the Integration method. Tools for that and several examples are in the next chapter. Sometimes Synthesis is possible. Less often the Fusion approach is employed, as it involves more taxing upfront effort for a longer-term payoff; that is, the investment of significant resources is made in anticipation of a conflict, rather than to address a current challenge. But Fusion can yield powerful results.

Figures 5.2, 5.3, and 5.4 apply the problem–conflict–contradiction–paradox model as discussed in Chapter 4 to three classic family problems. The tables – 5.2, 5.3, and 5.4 – present all six paradox management approaches discussed in this chapter, as applied to three of the classic family business conflicts presented in Chapter 4: family employment (discussed throughout this chapter), dividend or distribution policy, and family meetings. Studying these closely will deepen understanding and enhance application of the paradox management continuum.

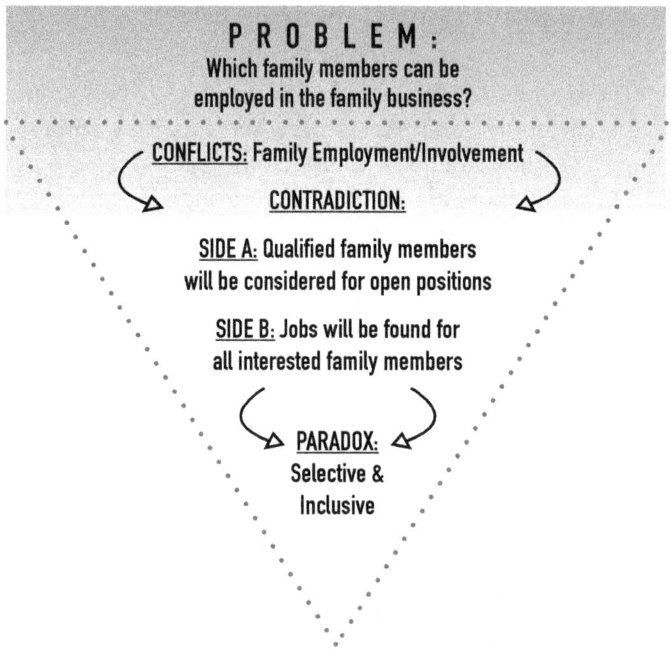


**Figure 5.2** *Family employment*

**Table 5.2** *Family employment: application of paradox management*

| Type | Continuum | Associated actions |
|---|---|---|
| Either/Or | Choice | **Business First**: Only well-qualified family members (e.g., at least three years of outside experience; advanced degree) will be considered for open positions<br>OR<br>**Family First**: Jobs will be found for all interested family members. |
| | Compromise | Family members are considered for employment after completing a minimum of two years outside work experience and a business-sponsored management education course. Minimizes possibility of unqualified, entitled, family employees, while relaxing requirements for those interested in joining. |
| | Balance | One member of each branch or couple encouraged to work in the business. Maximizes access to talent without overloading the business with family members. |
| Both/*AND* | Integration | Move beyond employment as the core conflict and seek appropriate family involvement opportunities in a variety of roles. Maximize both sides of the paradox: selectivity *and* inclusion. At the same time, manage weaknesses associated with each. Thus some roles will require more selectivity and careful matching between responsibilities and skills/experience. Other roles will support greater inclusivity by requiring fewer formal qualifications. |
| | Synthesis | Recognize the opportunity for *selective inclusion* and *inclusive selection* by pursuing practices that simultaneously promote inclusion and selectivity, for example:<br>❑ Instead of imposing a fixed set of rules – or no rules – on family employment, each interested family member is expected to conduct their own research into the relative merits of inclusive and selective approaches.<br>❑ The interested family member creates a personal action plan for how they would like to proceed and how they propose to manage potential weaknesses.<br>❑ The family business works with the family member to understand and implement the individual action plan within or outside the family business. |
| | Fusion | A systemic approach is implemented in anticipation of the paradox. For example, all family members (beginning at age 18) are encouraged to work with the Family HR committee to identify and develop their unique talents. The committee assists family members in multiple ways (e.g., testing, family history, education). As a result, family members naturally become involved in the aspect of the business that best fits their interests and skills and the enterprise's needs. |

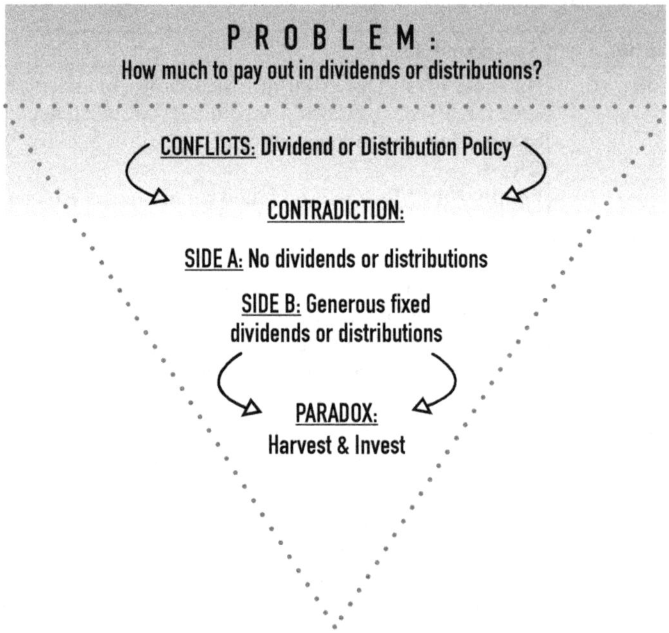


**Figure 5.3** *Dividend or distribution policy*

**Table 5.3** *Dividend/distribution policy: application of paradox management*

| Type | Continuum | Associated actions |
|---|---|---|
| Either/Or | Choice | **Business First**: No dividends/distributions<br>OR<br>**Family First**: Generous fixed dividends/distributions. |
| | Compromise | NYSE companies pay out approximately 30–35 percent of net profit; private companies often have no specific obligation. Families frequently split the difference and return 10 percent to 15 percent. This approach minimizes weaknesses of the choices available. |
| | Balance | Family receives a minimum fixed amount annually, plus an additional 25 percent of net profit above a 10 percent return, smoothed over a three-year rolling average. This approach maximizes opportunities. |
| Both/AND | Integration | Move beyond dividends/distributions as the core conflict and seek to maximize both sides of the paradox – harvest *and* invest – while managing weaknesses of each. In this case, directors might establish an annual dividend/distribution based upon both the business's needs for funding *and* the owners' rights to a return on their capital investment. Target dividend/distribution payout ratio is established, not in a fixed manner, but in a way that adapts to changing conditions each year and seeks to harvest *and* invest. |
| | Synthesis | "Can't harvest without investment, can't invest without harvesting." The expectation of regular ownership dividends/distributions emboldens management to take "more powerful" risks to grow the business with well-placed capital investments. In turn, effective capital investments assure regular ownership dividends/distributions. |
| | Fusion | A systemic approach is implemented in anticipation of the paradox: owners and managers establish policies that provide the freedom for owners to access investment value while incorporating commitment to invest in the future of the family business. Shareholder agreements that facilitate sale of shares and loan programs allowing owners to access share value without requiring redemption yields owners who don't feel "trapped" by their shares and are more likely to support long-term investment, often at the sacrifice of their own short-term dividends/distributions. |

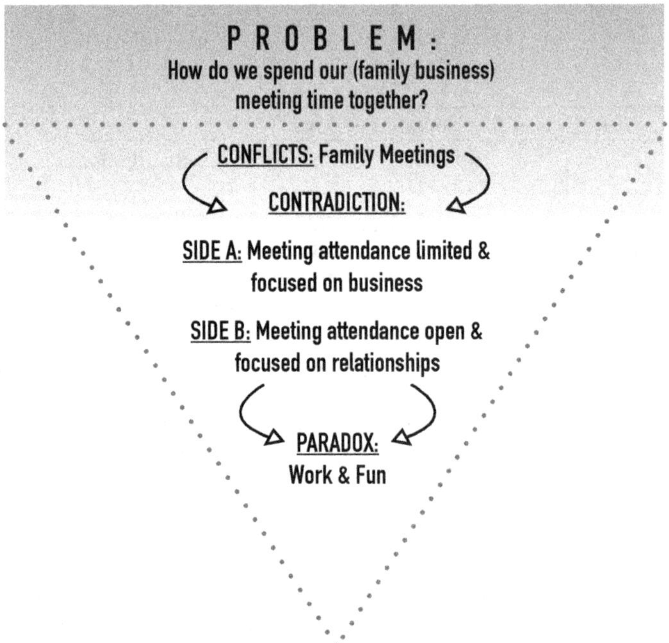


**Figure 5.4** *Family meetings*

**Table 5.4** *Family meeting: application of paradox management*

| Type | Continuum | Example associated actions |
|---|---|---|
| Either/Or | Choice | **Business First**: Business discussions dominate the agenda<br>OR<br>**Family First**: Relationship discussions dominate the agenda. |
| | Compromise | Family members required to attend at least one meeting focused on business and one meeting focused on relationships each quarter. This approach minimizes weaknesses. |
| | Balance | Family meetings have many different aspects (1/3 fun, 1/3 education, 1/3 business) but not all family members are expected to attend all parts of the meeting – they attend the parts that interest them. This approach maximizes opportunities. |
| Both/AND | Integration | Move beyond meetings as the core conflict and seek to maximize both sides of the paradox – fun *and* work – while minimizing the weaknesses of each.<br>❑ Family members participate in all aspects of the meeting – from planning to execution and evaluation. They understand the importance and value of both fun *and* work. Agendas seek to maximize both sides of fun *and* work.<br>❑ Meetings impart important business and family information, and are valued by all. Creative educational approaches engage all generations of owners (e.g., Monopoly, relay races, or scavenger hunts are focused on the history and other aspects of the business *and* the family). |
| | Synthesis | Achieve both sides of the paradox simultaneously: "Work can be fun, and fun entails plenty of work." Efforts go well beyond family meetings: for example, involvement in and attendance at "important moments" (e.g., store openings, recognition ceremonies for customers, vendors or employees, charitable donations) allows family simultaneously to enjoy the privileges and fulfill the responsibilities of ownership. |
| | Fusion | The paradox of work *and* fun evolves into a guiding principle: "Work is fun." The family seeks multiple opportunities to live this principle. Likely, another paradox emerges: responsibility *and* privilege.<br>❑ Knowledgeable family members become advocates for the family and the business, both internally to the business and externally to other family business/industry/customer forums. Family teams are invited to talk about the family and business – they build their presentation skills and knowledge of family business and forge unique relationships with stakeholder groups.<br>❑ The family benchmarks and shares best practices with other family businesses with similar traditions and value structures. They host other families and share experiences/best practices as they become a role-model family business. |

## CYCLE OF RENEWAL AND BENEFIT

Families investing the time and care to apply paradox management approaches gain in ways beyond making progress on the problem at hand. They learn to respect the variety of views within the family. Few values serve families better than mutual respect. Families also learn to find paradoxes among their problems, and they come to see the potential within the paradox. When a paradox is uncovered and deemed worthy of addressing – to derive benefit from both its inherent truths – families must gain the insight and skills to apply more heuristic, or Both/*AND*, approaches to the paradox. Taking this approach dramatically increases the slope of potential benefits gained from paradox management.

Continuing practice and skill at paradox management strengthens the enthusiasm to apply the methods and strengthens family bonds, ultimately creating a "cycle of renewal and benefit" at the right side of the continuum, as shown in Figure 5.5. As the family grows and moves through succeeding generations, their approach to the continuum must also grow and develop: monitoring and revamping tactics for managing a given paradox is essential as the family business context changes. Carried out thoughtfully, each application of paradox management creates greater benefits for the family and the business, renewing commitment to both.

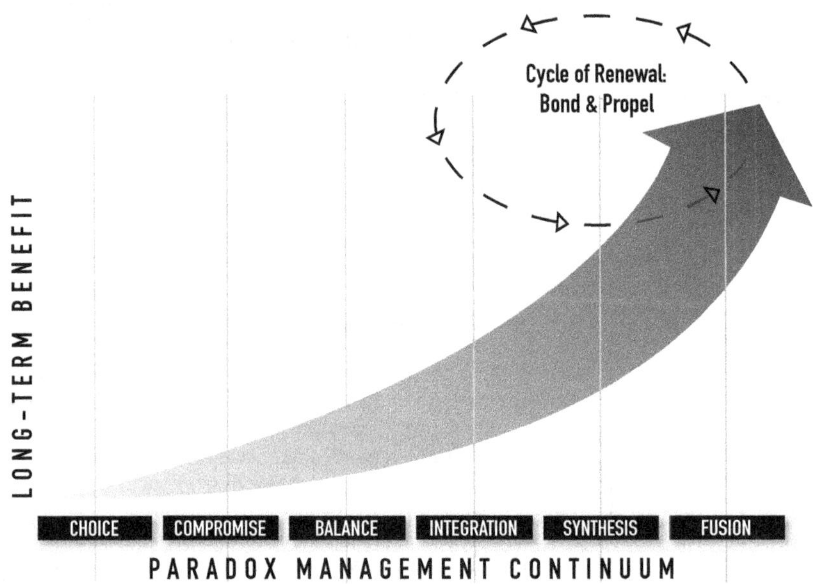


**Figure 5.5** *Paradox management cycle of renewal*

# 6 One Key Tool: The Polarity Map™

As challenging as paradox management can be, families and businesses across the globe have found methods for understanding and addressing them successfully.

> The phenomenon of interdependent opposites (dilemma, paradox, polarity) has been written about in philosophy and religion for over 4,000 years. It is a central reality in all of life and all human systems. It has only been in the last 20 years that it has been explicitly identified by business and industry as an important dimension to pay attention to because tapping the power of this dimension of life gives a competitive advantage.[1]
>
> Dr. Barry Johnson, Polarity Management Associates

The previous chapter detailed a continuum for the management of paradox from Either/Or to Both/*AND*, across six approaches. This chapter introduces a proven process for addressing the challenges and opportunities presented by paradoxes. The Polarity Map™ is an especially useful tool for achieving Integration on the paradox management continuum. Much of this chapter is drawn from workshops and materials developed by Dr. Johnson and Polarity Management Associates.[2]

## ANNA'S FAMILY BUSINESS AND POLARITY MAPPING

The following case example concerns a third-generation global food-related business operated by a large Greek family; it is based on several family businesses, to provide a context for building a Polarity Map™.

The family has used the concepts of paradox management and polarity mapping extensively to handle myriad issues covered over a decade of family meetings, as discussed by Anna, the family's matriarch. "I learned to live with the Both/*AND*," Anna said. She went on say:

> I can see the great progress our family has made, and at the same time, all the ways that we still need to grow and develop. Years ago, it would have been very difficult for me to accept that both of these facts are true. I was raised in a very Either/Or household, and never experienced a Both/*AND* mindset. The family meeting process has shown that to me.

Related to this notion, Anna recalled a conversation from several years ago:

> I was feeling very sad about the distance between me and my eldest daughter. She had chosen to live far away and we only saw each other once a year, at Christmas. Even with the distance, we continued to experience great closeness. I felt my customary Either/Or mindset struggling with this reality. How was it possible that she had chosen to live so far away, that we saw each other so seldom, and yet we still felt so closely bonded? I was able to recognize this as yet another example of the Both/AND. I could relax and accept the reality of the situation, which was something new for me.

Anna described a raft of experiences she remembered from years of family meetings, where she often felt two ostensibly contradictory emotions at the same time: pride in her grandchildren and disappointment with them; warmth and acceptance towards her son-in-law, fear of him, and anger at him. For Anna, recognizing this dual nature of reality was freeing, and she related it to important developments in the family's capacity to act as strong, capable stewards of their family business:

> When I was growing up, my parents would not tolerate disagreement or conflict. They also could not tolerate differences between people. The Both/AND would have been a very difficult concept for my parents to grasp. Since we weren't allowed to express disagreement with each other, we rarely expressed what we really felt to each other. Consequently, the decisions we made were not truly reflective of what we thought and felt, and more intense conflict would pop out at unexpected moments! We lived in a state of uncertainty, never knowing when these unexpressed disagreements would explode onto the scene. Paradoxically, living in the Both/*AND* makes me feel more secure about our decisions. They are based on reality, not fantasy or wishes.

In discussing her experience in her family business, Anna pointed out how hard the family had worked to prepare for the transition to the next generation. For example, they had developed a summer internship program and family employment policy; several teens from the next generation had participated in the internship program, to their benefit and that of the business. "We never would have had a program like this in the past," Anna said:

> My father was skeptical of the involvement of family members. He was afraid they would interfere with his ability to run the business. My husband, the founder's son-in-law, became CEO in the second generation. It was the best solution for us because choosing among siblings for succession would have been too hard. But we'd like to do it differently for our children. This is another example of the Both/AND for us – we want to introduce the next generation to their business in a way that respects both the needs of the business and the needs of the family, rather than making an Either/Or choice.

For Anna's family, implementing the Both/AND has included the use of polarity mapping. This technique explores deeply the two sides that comprise a paradox – or a "polarity," as it called in Dr. Barry Johnson's work – in ways that help maximize the upsides and minimize the downsides of each side. As such, it is a way of carrying out the Integration approach of the paradox management continuum from Chapter 5. The next sections detail the specific steps involved in polarity mapping, through the example of how Anna's family business created an internship program.

## Assemble a group and identify the poles (Steps 1 and 2)

The first step in completing a Polarity Map™ is to assemble the appropriate set of people to work on it. For Anna, the group was comprised of family members, with input from the company's HR staff. The group must get to work by identifying the two interdependent values (or sides, or poles) at play. For the issue of the family internship, Anna's family called the two sides "An internship that is supportive of the business" and "An internship that is supportive of the family," as portrayed in Figure 6.1.

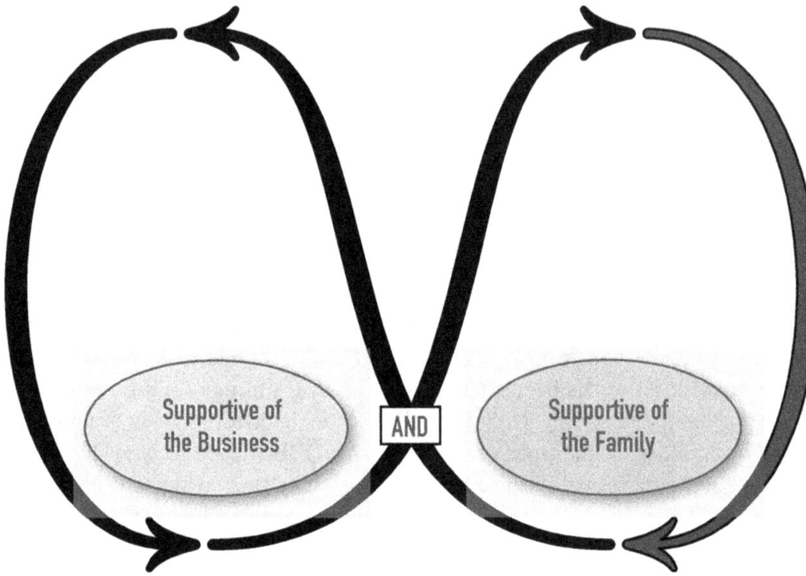


**Figure 6.1** *Family internship example: name the poles (sides)*

It is important to use positive, desirable values in naming the two sides. The map is not meant to be composed of two sides that are "opposite" in the traditional sense. For example, it would not be useful to think of the two poles in this case as "Support the business" and "Harm the business," or "Honor the needs of the family" and "Ignore the needs of the family." The sides should reflect their positive aspects.

## List upsides and downsides (Step 3)

Once two sides (or values) have been identified and named, the group must begin thinking about the upsides associated with each, and list them in the corresponding upper quadrant (as in Figure 6.2). Note that upsides are not meant to be the "pros" of each side. In Anna's case, in this stage the group used as a guide the two questions "What are the benefits of creating an internship that supports the family?" and "What are the benefits of creating an internship that supports the business?" The group placed their answers to these questions in the two associated *Upsides* quadrants in the Polarity Map™ as depicted in Figure 6.2.

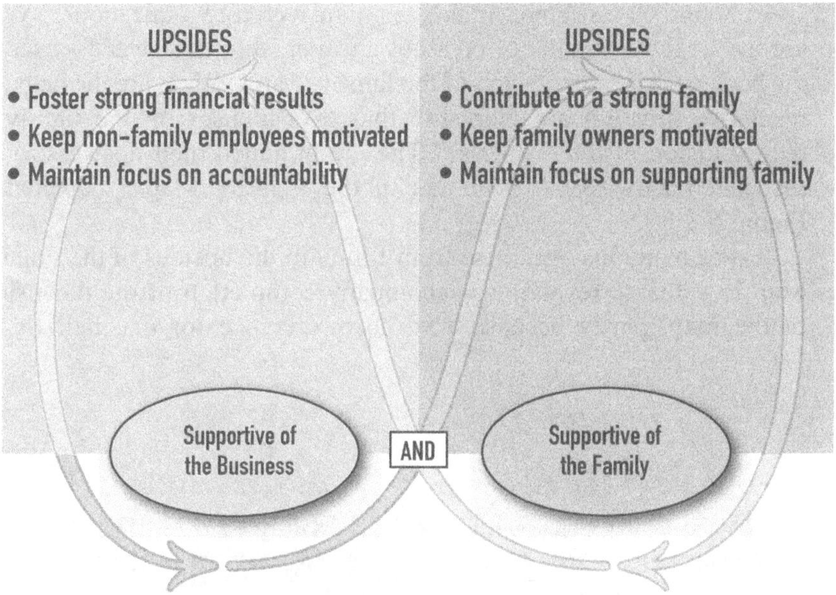


**Figure 6.2** *Family internship example: list upsides*

Considering the upsides of each value is, by definition, a Both/*AND* approach. No matter how much one side might be preferred, completing a Polarity Map™ forces awareness of the benefits of both sides of the paradox. In this way, the process builds understanding and respect for a position that may, in the past, have seemed foreign or in clear opposition to the business's or family's established practices. Similarly, it provides a forum for individuals whose point of view may not have been fully heard or understood in the past. Finally, it creates a platform of open discussion that moves everyone in a beneficial and mutually supportive direction, as the conversation is focused on the situation, rather than individual people.

Because the Polarity Map™ approach is grounded in realism, it also recognizes the need to explore the shadow sides – or potential downsides – of each value, in addition to its upsides. So the group creating the map must next brainstorm the negative results of *over-focusing* on one pole. Note that this is not about discussing the cons of this side. Rather, the map is constructed to reflect the extreme case, where one pole is ignored in service of the other, and vice versa.

To approach this step, Anna's team answered two questions: "What are the negative results of creating an internship that over-focuses on the business to the exclusion of the family?" and "What are the negative results of creating an internship that over-focuses on the family to the exclusion of the business?" The group added their answers to the associated *Downsides* quadrants in the Polarity Map™ depicted in Figure 6.3.

Just as many insights arise from filling in the upsides of the Polarity Map™, valuable revelations accompany completion of the downsides of the map, partly because a strong preference for one half of the

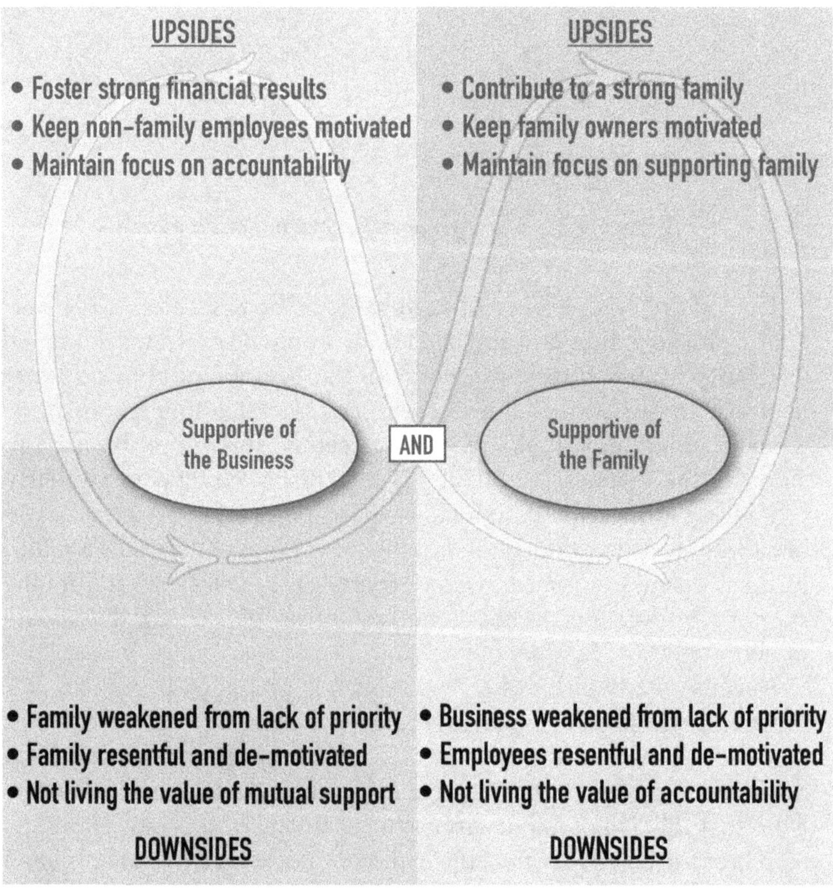


**Figure 6.3** *Family internship example: list downsides*

polarity often means blindness to its downsides. Conversely, through this process a group can also find evidence that it has been over-emphasizing, even demonizing, the downside of the pole that is not preferred. As with many business endeavors, the means are more important than the ends: those participating in the process of creating the map benefit from listening, understanding, and gaining consensus about how to capture and ultimately manage the issue at hand.

## Appreciate the infinity loop (Step 4)

The shape and construction of the Polarity Map™ is not accidental. It is deliberately constructed on a grid to demonstrate the predictable movement between the two poles or two sides of the paradox. Specifically, movement through the Polarity Map™ traces the shape of an infinity loop, cycling from one side of the grid to the other in a broad, arcing movement between the two. The movement can start anywhere on the map; but the most natural place to start is the upside of the pole preferred by an individual or the group. In that case, the infinity loop would begin at the upside of one value and move to that pole's downside, then in a diagonal movement to the upside of the other pole, to that pole's downside, then in a similar diagonal movement to the upside of the opposite pole, thus returning to where it began.

This infinity loop represents the natural flow between the two poles. The movement never stops, although its shape (its height and width) will vary widely by time and situation. One might think that the "best" place to be on the Polarity Map™ is within the upside of the preferred pole. However, since movement within the map is inevitable, trying to stay permanently within either upside is impossible. Further, over-emphasizing one side will inevitably over time push the business to the downside of that value. By consciously seeking actions and approaches that reinforce both poles, one can minimize the time spent in both downsides. Thus the desired "steady state" would be described as productive movement in an infinity loop between the two poles, focused primarily on the upsides of both poles, while spending minimum time and energy on their downsides.

The sample Polarity Map™ in Figure 6.3 illustrates how a family business might move naturally through the infinity loop. Indeed, Anna and her family business moved between the two poles when they constructed their family internship program. Her husband Albert, the CEO, began the process by expressing the importance of putting the business first when creating the internship. According to Albert, focusing on the business would help him continue to attract and retain strong non-family employees and create a culture of accountability. Through these statements, Albert positioned his approach firmly in the upside of the business-first value – supportive of the business.

However, as Albert spoke about maintaining a focus on the business, many family members became uncomfortable. They began to worry that Albert would accept only an internship that emphasized the needs of the business – to the exclusion of the family's needs. This approach could demotivate next-generation family members and cause them to feel unsupported by the business. The internship program Albert envisioned would likely weaken the connection between the family and the business, and as such represented a step in the wrong direction.

This approach made Anna's sister Kate particularly uncomfortable. From a very young age, Kate's eldest son had been interested in the business and sought opportunities to work there. Not surprisingly, Kate gravitated to the upside of the family-focus value: she advocated an internship program that would warmly welcome family members interested in the business. She also suggested that a family-focused internship would create strong connections between the family and the business, and strengthen the family along the way. Yet the more Kate talked about the advantages of a strong family-focused internship program, the more worried Albert felt about undue family presence. He was concerned that such a program would place unnecessary burdens on his employees, distracting them from their jobs and maybe even weakening the culture of accountability he had worked so hard to reinforce.

Albert's and Kate's discrepant perceptions demonstrate how a family moves through the four quadrants of a Polarity Map™. Neither position is right or wrong; there is truth and wisdom in both values. Keeping this in mind, Anna's family moved through the Polarity Map™ and designed an internship that honored both family *and* business. In the process, Albert and Kate were both able to appreciate the importance of the set of principles that seemed opposite their own.

Paradoxically, to the extent that one value on the map is emphasized over the other, the group will be pushed even more strongly to the downside of the emphasized pole. So the more that Kate pushed for a family-first internship, the more members of the group articulated the advantages of focusing on the business's needs. When Kate stepped back and acknowledged the importance of the business's needs, the family eased up on defending the business against her perceived lack of sensitivity.

However, as the group began to emphasize more strongly an internship that focused on the business in order to maintain strong financial performance and retain motivated and talented non-family employees, the group became uncomfortable with the business-first approach. They worried that it would create greater distance between the family and the business, and that the lack of attention to the family would result in a weaker and more dependent family. Awareness of the downside of focusing too exclusively on the business propelled the group naturally to the upside of focusing on the family.

This movement from one pole to the other in a Polarity Map™ is natural and indeed inevitable; it cannot be stopped. Moreover, the movement is of a positive, corrective nature, and thus it would be unwise to attempt to block it. Maintaining a focus on both poles (as part of a Both/*AND* approach) moderates the degree of oscillation between poles. Over-focusing on one pole for a longer period of time will result in a wider and deeper swing to the other. So, taking deliberate steps to maintain focus on both poles is important.

## Identify Action Steps and Early Warnings (Step 5)

The next two steps in constructing a Polarity Map™ help the group deliberately maintain focus on both poles. The steps involve identifying Action Steps associated with both upsides and Early Warnings associated with both downsides.

Action Steps, in this example, represent specific steps the family can take to create an internship that supports both the business *and* the family. These are to be listed beside the upside of each pole. Similarly, Early Warnings are identified and noted beside each of the two downsides. They describe "red flags" that can alert the group to the fact

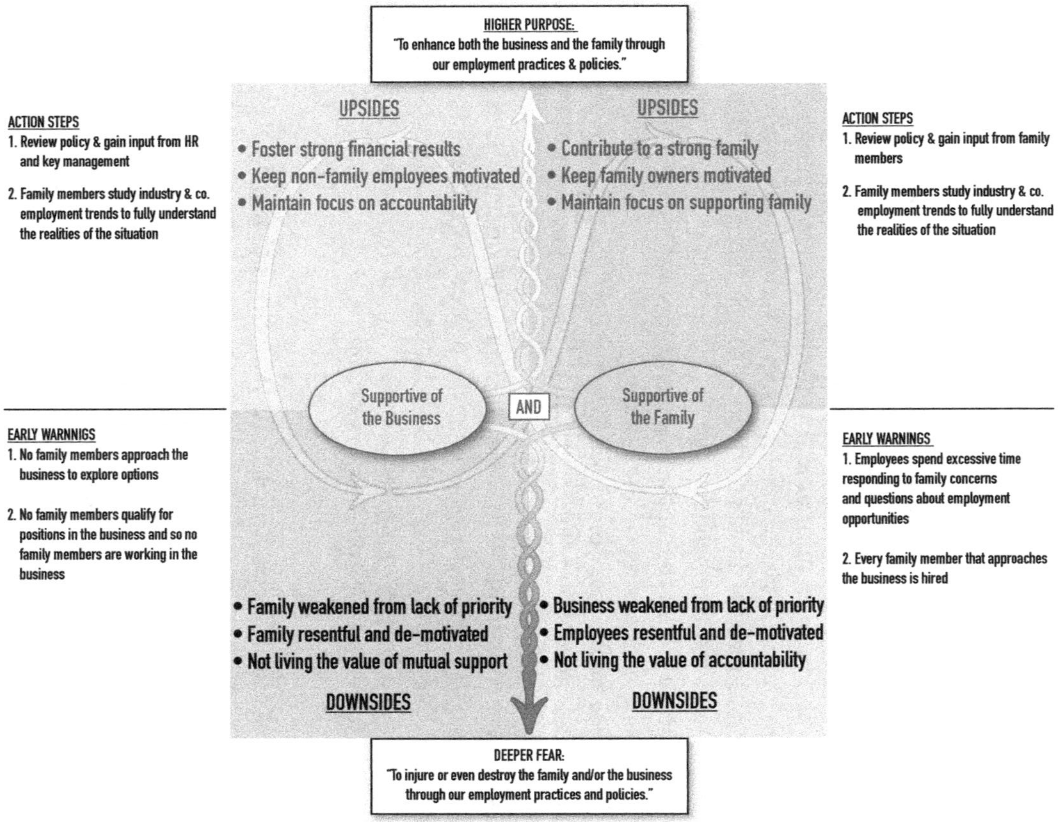


**Figure 6.4** *Family internship: complete Polarity Map™*

that the internship may be over-focused on a particular pole. Figure 6.4 depicts the Action Steps and Early Warnings for Anna's family's map. Note that these two steps are not always necessary for completing the map, but identifying Action Steps and Early Warnings typically makes the mapping even more complete and illuminating. They also provide the group with specific actions for achieving Integration.

Take a close look at the Action Steps on the map in Figure 6.4. It may be surprising to see one action that's common to both upsides: "Family members study industry and company employment trends to fully understand the realities of the situation." This is considered a "high-leverage action step" because it promotes the upsides of both poles. In the example, this step is supportive of the family, because it provides members with the opportunity to learn more about the realities of employment in both their company *and* their broader industry, positioning them to be more effective in their careers within or outside the company. At the same time, this step is supportive of the business, because it ensures that internship policies are created with industry-wide *and* business-specific trends in mind, thus better supporting the business's needs.

## Create Higher Purpose and Deeper Fear statements (Step 6)

At this point, two steps remain to complete the map: filling in the map's Higher Purpose statement and Deeper Fear statement. In some cases, these can be the very first items placed on the map; in others, they emerge later, as the group gains more insight from filling in the other sections. The Higher Purpose describes the ultimate reason to manage the polarity, answering the question "What is the overall goal we are trying to achieve by understanding and managing this polarity?" The Deeper Fear describes the negative outcome that all are striving to prevent – it answers the question "What is the overall result that we want to prevent by understanding and managing this polarity?" In this example, the Greater Purpose statement is "To enhance both the business and the family through our employment practices and policies." The Deeper Fear statement is "To injure or even destroy the family and/or the business through our employment practices and policies." The map in Figure 6.4 includes these statements as well, and is now complete.

## Promote virtuous cycles; prevent vicious cycles (Step 7)

Polarity Maps™ offer an important advantage to those who take the time to complete them. In addition to the benefits already discussed, the map can reveal the presence of virtuous and vicious cycles, indicated by the spiraling arrows along the vertical axis on the map in Figure 6.4. A virtuous cycle is present when the family's efforts are centered predominantly on the upsides of both poles, which is also the goal of the Integration approach on the paradox management continuum. The family is actively pursuing both sides of the paradox, consistently and deliberately, over a long period. If they find themselves over-emphasizing one pole to the exclusion of the other, they quickly take self-correcting steps. When both sides of a paradox are actively pursued in this way, experience of the downsides is minimized, and the flow between the two sides of the paradox is smooth and productive.

Using Anna's family business case, an example of a virtuous cycle is when family members interested in the internship act in ways that are respectful of all the guidelines governing it: they don't ask for special treatment or consideration; they are timely and thorough in the application process. In this regard, they emphasize the needs of the business. In turn, the behavior of employees at the business reflects the virtuous cycle if they are timely and thorough in responding to family members and discharging their responsibilities with regard to the internship; in this way, they emphasize the needs of the family. Such professional and respectful behavior on the part of family and employees of the business promotes feelings of warmth and support within the system. Each virtuous action leads to the next set of virtuous actions. Each positive experience builds the foundation for the next. By fully understanding and respecting the needs of both business *and* family, all those involved foster a deep sense of trust and respect. A virtuous cycle may be difficult to start in the first place; but once the attitudes, practices, and policies promoting it are established, it is easier to maintain, given its self-reinforcing nature.

Conversely, family businesses may find themselves stuck in the downsides of both poles, in a vicious cycle. For example, members of Anna's family might have acted as if they were entitled to special treatment as applicants and/or interns, pulling HR employees and others away from their job responsibilities; thus they would have failed to respect the needs of the business. Such behavior would likely have been met with resentment and protectiveness on the part of employees involved: they could have been late or incomplete in their responses to the family, thus failing to respect the family's needs. The family members involved may have reacted with increasing frustration, and possibly even suspicion that the employees were seeking to keep them out of the business. It's easy to see how such a vicious cycle can arise, gain strength, and perpetuate itself over time.

So what is the solution to a vicious cycle? Quite simply, it is to take steps to pay explicit attention to both poles and maximize their upsides. In very short order, the dynamic then shifts from a competition for scarce resources to cooperation for ample resources. Attending to the insights and awareness conveyed by the map makes this transition much more likely.

## Engage in group reflection and learning (Step 8)

As mentioned earlier, the Polarity Map™ is best completed by a group of stakeholders who are most knowledgeable of or affected by the situation being analyzed. In the Polarity Map™ for Anna's family's internship program, that is the group suggested earlier: family members and key individuals from HR. They would learn valuable insights just from collaborating to draft the map. Again, the process is more about bringing stakeholders together to achieve mutual understanding than about the completed map.

Completing a Polarity Map™ takes significant time and thoughtfulness. At this point, it makes sense to step back and ask, "What does all this time, effort and analysis give me?" The answer is simple. The Polarity Map™ is a tool that supports a full exploration and understanding of the two seemingly opposing, interdependent sides that make up a paradox. It is an especially helpful tool for the paradox management continuum's Integration approach. The downsides of ignoring either side are confronted, along with the advantages of pursuing the benefits of both.

A Polarity Map™ reveals both personal and group preferences. Many times, when completing a map, a group has a very difficult time listing upsides for one of the poles – in extreme cases, a group may not be able to list a single upside. For example, a family looking at the business first *and* family first paradox with a strong preference for the business-first pole (perhaps they have historically been worried about unqualified family members coming to work in the business) may have a hard time coming up with any upsides for the family-first pole, because of their fears and anxieties. However, if the family pushes itself to see the potential upsides of both poles, it could open itself to an entire universe of possibilities it had been blind to before.

How did this play out in Anna's family's case? In completing the Polarity Map™, her sister Kate realized that she seldom thought about the needs of the business, believing that the business was large and strong enough to find a place for any family member seeking an internship, no matter what their level of skill was. Completing the map fostered in Kate a deep and sincere understanding of the importance of accounting for the business's needs in developing a family internship. Albert, the business's CEO and Anna's husband, who entered the conversation with tremendous worry that the internship would engender a sense of family entitlement, came to a deeper appreciation for the benefits of having family members with direct experience with the business they owned, including using their passion and interest to enhance energy levels and cohesion within the business.

## THE CONTINUUM AND THE MAP

The polarity mapping process helped Kate, Albert, and other family members to let go of many of their fears regarding the internship. The internship they eventually created explicitly honored the needs of both the family *and* the business, and was a great success. As suggested earlier, it is an example of the Integration level on the paradox management continuum (see Figure 6.5), an approach that seeks to maximize the opportunities and minimize the weaknesses of both sides. The Polarity Map™ can be a vital tool for Both/*AND* thinking. The process of mapping a polarity can also reveal possibilities at the next level of this type of thinking: Synthesis. Synthesis involves finding ways to address both sides simultaneously. The high-leverage action step (in other words, having family members study industry and business-specific trends) discovered while creating Anna's family's map is an example of a step

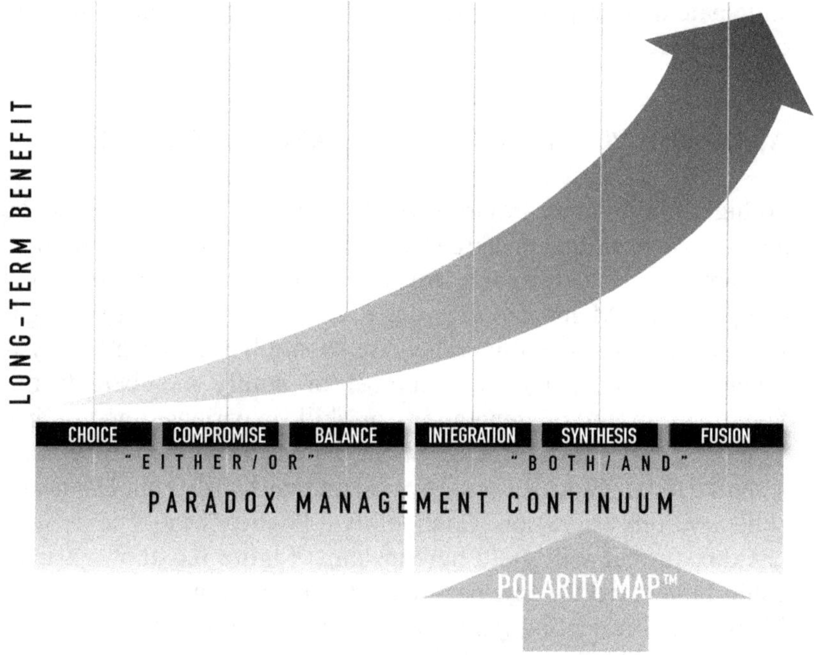


**Figure 6.5** *Paradox management continuum*

toward Synthesis, because it served the needs of the family and the business simultaneously.

Further, families that spend sufficient time understanding and actively managing the paradoxes they face build a level of skill and understanding that can help them to achieve the level of Fusion on the paradox management continuum – the highest Both/*AND* approach. For Anna's family, a state of Fusion could be represented by the development of a whole array of family and business education that would begin when family members are as young as 5 or 10 years of age. In this scenario, the younger family members would likely hear the reports of older children who have undertaken internships. Those accounts might include an assessment by the participants regarding how an optimal balance of family-focused and business-focused values was achieved. The conversations might also address an analysis of the possible virtuous and vicious cycles in the internship program. Deeper Fusion might be achieved by using the internship to help members anticipate and prepare for future roles as family business owners and/or employees.

## ANOTHER POLARITY MAP™: FAMILY COUNCILS

To highlight how the Polarity Map™ can help family business groups address longstanding disagreements and tensions while promoting both the family *and* the business, consider another example: family council composition. Many families have strong disagreements regarding whether family council membership should be based on family representation (that is, a certain number of family members from each family group and/or generation) or skill, experience, and/or interest. When examined as a paradox rather than as a problem to be solved or a choice to be made, it becomes evident that family councils need both skills *and* representation. Completing a Polarity Map™ to explore this paradox further will yield new insights. Figure 6.6 shows a map that could be created for this paradox; of course, your group's map would likely differ, reflecting features of your specific situation.

The map clearly shows the truth and value contained in both sides, and the hazards of emphasizing one side to the exclusion of the other. This is why many of the strongest family councils focus on both representative and skill-based membership. One family, for example, aims to have at least one council member from each generation, and ideally each branch. But they combine this approach with a focus on skill and experience – ensuring that at least one council member has tremendous leadership and facilitation skills, one has passion for the family's history, one is experienced with programming for children (to develop family career development programs, for example), and so on. This solution may initially be more complicated, but it taps the wisdom of both representation-focused *and* skills-based approaches. Overall, it represents an approach that is neither simplistic nor unnecessarily complicated.

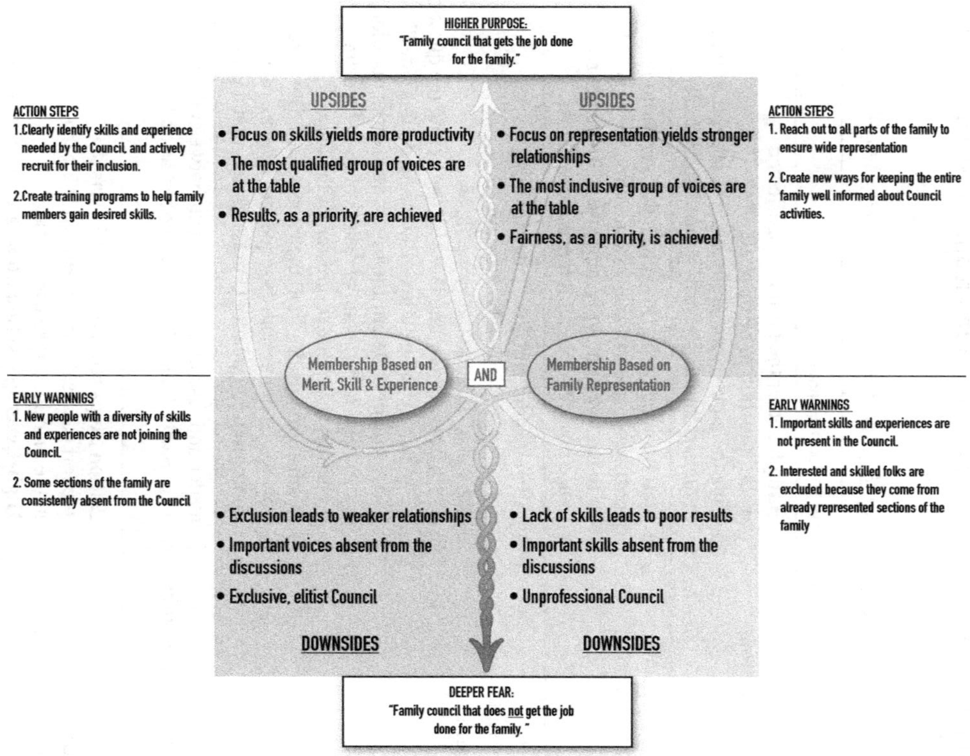


**Figure 6.6** *Family council composition Polarity Map™*

## STEP BY STEP THROUGH THE POLARITY MAP™

Every group will approach the mapping process differently, and different areas of focus benefit different situations. Table 6.1 presents a set of guidelines for completing a Polarity Map™, with the understanding that each group's experience in creating a specific map will be unique.

**Table 6.1** *Step by step through the Polarity Map™*

| Mapping process step | How to implement |
|---|---|
| Step 1:<br>Assemble a group | ❑ Bring together the group most affected by the situation to be mapped.<br>❑ Give the group some grounding in concepts of paradox in general and the Polarity Map™ specifically. |
| Step 2:<br>Identify the poles | ❑ Start by naming the two values that appear to be conflicting; upon further examination, they should be found to be mutually supportive. Remember to use positive or neutral terms for the sides. |
| Step 3:<br>List upsides and downsides | ❑ Fill in upsides and downsides for both poles– the order will be determined by the particular situation the group faces.<br>– **Upsides**: Determine these by answering the question "What are the benefits of focusing on this side?"<br>– **Downsides**: Determine by answering the question "What are the negative results of over-focusing on this side to the exclusion of the other?"<br>❑ Brainstorm upsides first, then downsides. But note, however, that alternative sequences may be more appropriate; Appendix D presents additional examples. |
| Step 4:<br>Appreciate the infinity loop | Consider and discuss the movement between the two poles of the Polarity Map,™ often described as an "infinity loop." |
| Step 5:<br>Identify Action Steps and Early Warnings | ❑ **Action Steps** represent specific acts that support each side of the paradox. List these in the margin next to each upside.<br>❑ **High-Leverage Action Steps** are specific acts that support both sides of the paradox (in line with the paradox-continuum level Synthesis)<br>❑ **Early Warnings** represent "red flags," raising awareness that one pole is being ignored while the other pole receives excess focus. List these in the margin next to each downside. |

Table 6.1 continued

| | |
|---|---|
| Step 6:<br>Create Higher Purpose and Deeper Fear statements | ❑ **Higher Purpose statement**: Written at the map's top, this describes the ultimate reason for managing the paradox.<br>❑ **Deeper Fear statement**: Written at the map's bottom, this describes the negative outcome that all are striving to prevent through management of the paradox.<br>❑ These statements are often completed at the beginning of the process to create clear focus, or at the end to serve as simple summary statements. They can be completed at any time during the process. |
| Step 7:<br>Promote virtuous cycles; prevent vicious cycles | ❑ **Virtuous cycles** are entered into when the group's focus is predominantly in the upsides of both poles. This is achieved by actively pursuing both sides of the paradox – consistently and deliberately, over a long period. Experience of the downsides is minimized; flow between the two upsides is smooth and productive. Each positive, supportive action leads to the next.<br>❑ **Vicious cycles** occur when a group finds itself stuck in the downsides of both poles. This results from over-focusing on one side of the paradox to the exclusion of the other. This neglect of one side tends to center the group in the downsides of both poles. Destructive, unsupportive action tends to lead to such actions. Vicious cycles can be broken by ensuring focus on and respect for both sides of the paradox. |
| Step 8:<br>Engage in group reflection and learning | ❑ Reflect, discuss, grow – and enjoy the insights your map provides! |

## FINAL REFLECTIONS

As explored in this chapter, the Polarity Map™ offers very useful insights to groups grappling with paradoxes. A few notes in closing:

- ❑ Using neutral or positive words for each side of the paradox is essential in creating the conditions for a map that values both.
- ❑ Asking the group to name the sides together makes the map more interesting and relevant for them. If people outside the group

name the sides, the Polarity Map™ will tend to be less useful and powerful.

- Frequently, the sides won't be "opposites" in the traditional sense of the term. For example, a paradox where one side is loyalty might be identified to include freedom as the counterpart side, rather than disloyalty or betrayal. Similarly, the opposing value for freedom is not imprisonment.
- Describing the paradox with two positive sides increases the potential to "go beyond" Integration and achieve Synthesis or even Fusion.
- Regardless of the outcome of polarity mapping, going through the process will enhance the family's listening skills and mutual respect.

This chapter is intended to provide a basic introduction to the Polarity Map™, and to apply the tool to family business paradoxes. In Appendix D, the polarity map is applied to several other classic family business paradoxes, including privacy *and* transparency, and harvest *and* invest.

# Part IV

# Achieving Both

*This page intentionally left blank*

The significance of paradox management in our complex and challenging era is well recognized, as highlighted in a major, recent PriceWaterhouse study:

> A new "science" of management is emerging …. [Managers] will have to augment [their] competencies [technical, and analytical skills, perseverance and functional expertise] with instincts for balance and integration, and the ability to recognize and master nuance … key to success will be to approach management [in a way] that does not ignore or explain away the existence of contradictions and uncertainty – the existence of paradox … [Managers] will learn to balance deftly the paradoxes or points of tension that … run through their enterprises.[1]
>
> Price Waterhouse Change Integration Team, *The Paradox Principles*

Clearly, cultural attributes of famiy businesses shape their ability to manage paradox successfully, as will be explored in this final Part.

*This page intentionally left blank*

# 7 Experience the Power of Paradox

Once the results – and pleasure – of harnessing the power of paradox have been experienced, it can be difficult to go back to an exclusive focus on traditional problem-solving. Both/*AND* approaches, applied appropriately, are a compelling source of competitive advantage, and can become addictive.

> A belief is not merely an idea the mind possesses; it is an idea that possesses the mind.[1]
>
> Robert Bolton

One of this book's goals has been to demonstrate that family businesses must be prepared to solve traditional problems *and* to manage paradoxes. Traditional problem solving carries many rewards, whether deciding which new product to take to market, determining the dimensions of a corporate headquarters renovation, or selecting the next chair of the board. Therefore, skilled family enterprises will identify and manage paradoxes, in addition to solving problems, and can distinguish when each approach is needed.

## SOURCES OF CONTINUITY

Continuity across the generations is the overarching goal of most family businesses. This sense of purpose provides family businesses with the perspective, resolve, energy, and commitment to wrestle with the paradoxes they must confront on a regular basis. They seek to develop both the *capacity* and the *capability* to manage paradox well. In the Introduction, these concepts were defined as follows:

- ❑ **Capacity** to identify paradoxes and to understand and accept the ambiguity associated with them.
- ❑ **Capability** to use both sides of the paradox to generate greater insights and superior long-term results.

Both heuristic *and* algorithmic approaches are needed for success in this regard. The structure provided by algorithmic approaches, combined with the experimentation required by heuristic approaches, helps family businesses expand their capacity and capability for managing paradoxes. Family businesses have a head start: a tremendous ability to recognize the presence of paradoxes is built into their DNA.

Being part of a business family means that grandparents, parents, aunts and uncles, and even cousins are all too familiar with difficult, seemingly unsolvable contradictions. Perhaps they have sat together over coffee, confronting seemingly opposing needs among family members or family branches. Or they have spent late nights in conference rooms, struggling over conflicting requirements presented by stakeholders. Whatever the details, family businesses are able to recognize these dynamics when they arise. From day one, they know that accessing the energy inherent in paradoxes is an essential part of the family businesses environment; they have learned this through observations of, and interactions in, both the family and the business over the years.

In addition to having the capacity to recognize a paradox when they see it, most family businesses have also developed the needed skills and abilities, or capability, to manage paradoxes in a productive manner. This happens more often in family businesses because there is no room for anything less than a win–win solution when it comes to families in business together. Compromising business or family is not a viable option. The capability of family businesses to accept these tensions and seek Both/AND approaches can lead to success in both arenas. Although this knowledge or capability is not usually explicit, it is extremely useful. As more family businesses come to understand the concepts and techniques of paradox management, this implicit ability will become more explicit, and as a result, even more useful.

## CULTURE UNLOCKS THE POWER OF PARADOX

It is clear that some families and businesses do a very good job of managing paradoxes. For others, it is a constant struggle. Uncovering the presence of a paradox and working to harness the opportunities it contains appears to be enjoyable and fruitful for some organizations, but frustrating and less productive for others. A system's capacity for managing paradox is often shaped by its *culture*, which includes values, customs, traditions, and norms. What kinds of corporate and family cultures promote success in paradox management? What kinds of cultural attributes get in the way? A case example (based on a real-life example, with names and details changed) will help answer these questions.

### Bonner Construction

Meet Bruce Bonner, the third-generation CEO of a road construction company in Maine. Bruce's company has a no-nonsense approach to its business. It is lean, with a tiny central office supporting many dozens of project managers and road crews scattered across a wide geography. Bruce and his team rarely seek guidance from best-selling business books or high-profile management gurus. Instead, they rely heavily upon the wisdom of the two prior generations, whose leadership approach yielded decades of success. Upon closer examination, Bonner Construction has a corporate culture that is distinctly supportive of the Both/AND mindset required for successful paradox management.

Although not explicitly aware of his approach, Bruce successfully manages several key paradoxes when hiring new project managers. For example, in the hiring process, Bonner Construction's motto is "slow down to go fast." Although they have a reputation for being among the speediest and most thorough paving companies on the East Coast, when it comes to hiring, the firm deliberately slows down every aspect of the process. For instance, Bruce takes time to visit multiple engineering programs each year to personally interview newgraduates.

Since continuity has always been a major motivation of the Bonner family, the company has historically taken a careful approach to hiring, seeking solid contributors likely to build lifetime careers with the company. The selection process extends over several months, and includes both formal and informal interviews. By the time Bonner Construction extends a job offer to a new hire, Bruce Bonner and his team have personally spent the equivalent of at least three full days with the candidate, doing everything they can to determine whether he or she is a fit for the company.

Bruce actively manages the tension between decisive *and* deliberate decision making around new hires. By deliberately drawing out the hiring process, Bruce makes sure that a comprehensive set of data points are brought to the table before a decision is made. However, once the hiring offer has been made, the process moves quickly and decisively. Specific work assignments and packed training schedules are drawn up, in order to put the new hire to work as quickly and effectively as possible.

Bruce also manages the tension between attending to people *and* attending to projects. There is no question that Bonner Construction pays attention to projects, with a laser-sharp focus on getting jobs done on time and on budget. However, with his close, personal attention to hiring, Bruce shows an appreciation for the importance of attending to people as well. This approach to hiring began decades ago, with Bruce's father and grandfather, who also were deeply involved in recruiting for management positions.

Finally, Bruce and his team have learned that data are not the only important factors in hiring. By spending both formal *and* informal time with candidates – taking them out for lunch and spending plenty of time riding to job sites in the car – Bruce supplements his assessment of the candidates' resumes and credentials with his gut reaction to the candidate's interpersonal skills. The crews at Bonner Construction spend many long weeks together in remote stretches of Maine, so getting along with team mates is just as important for a project manager as having strong technical skills. Both sides are factored into the hiring decision, thus helping the Bonner team manage the paradox of gut-based decision making *and* data-based decision making.

In these ways, Bonner Construction provides an example of a corporate culture that gracefully manages several paradoxes present in the hiring process. Although this approach has never been made explicit, the family and the business have a history of accepting the inherent complexity of multiple paradoxes and managing them patiently, rather than jumping to solutions likely to create more problems than they solve.

## Optimal cultural conditions

In this book's Introduction, four foundational factors were highlighted as necessary to developing the capacity and capability to manage paradoxes. These factors are:

- ❑ Recognize that the issue the paradox represents is distinct from a typical business problem.
- ❑ Appreciate and accept the ambiguity and uncertainty inherent in paradox; resist the rush to resolve.
- ❑ Accept – even appreciate – the inherent tension and energy contained in the two seemingly opposite sides of the paradox.
- ❑ Develop the skills and abilities needed to manage paradoxes successfully.

How can the culture of the business and family best integrate these four factors into everyday life? Some family businesses have developed approaches – in both the family and the business – that are naturally supportive of paradox management. For these families, Integration and Synthesis are part and parcel of their daily discourse and decision making – it's just the way they do business. What do the cultures of such family businesses have in common? The following cultural conditions are consistently found in these family businesses (this list is not meant to be exhaustive):

- ❑ Compelling curiosity
- ❑ Long-term perspective
- ❑ World-class problem solving
- ❑ Solid trust
- ❑ Extensive communication.

### *Cultural condition 1: Compelling curiosity*

Families and businesses that manage paradox well tend to be very curious rather than judgmental. When confronted with new, challenging information or situations, rather than jumping to quick conclusions, they tend to respond with questions. This does not mean that they are incapable of making judgments or critiques. Rather, because of their curious culture, they tend to steer clear of rendering absolute opinions or broad generalizations based on limited information.

In these cultures, criticism tends to be constructive, rather than destructive. Individuals first seek to understand before reaching final conclusions. Data gathering and listening are a way of life in such environments. Questions abound, proclamations are rare. The norms – or informal rules governing behavior – emphasize mutual understanding. Table 7.1 contrasts more Judgmental Cultures with more Curious Cultures. The latter are significantly more conducive to managing paradox.

**Table 7.1** *Sample cultural attributes comparison*

| | **Judgmental Cultures (less conducive to managing paradox)** | **Curious Cultures (more conducive to managing paradox)** |
|---|---|---|
| **Values** | Focus on practices, not beliefs | Regularly reaffirmed and reinforced |
| **Norms** | Emphasis on right and wrong | Emphasis on mutual understanding |
| **Communication approach** | Asserting and making statements | Listening and asking questions |
| **Self-description** | "Our family is not like other families – we are special in so many ways" | "Our family is like most other families – although we do have special opportunities and burdens" |

We might ask whether family businesses tend to be more or less curious than widely held companies. There's no simple answer. As noted throughout this book, family businesses are more inclined to manage paradoxes well because of their history and perspectives, but not in all cases. Some families with a more judgmental culture, may have a tendency to place people and ideas on a pedestal. This often begins with the company founder, who is portrayed as being larger than life. In general, family myths may idolize the founding generation, and family members who do not always explicitly embody the founder's characteristics and habits may be judged adversely.

Other business-owning families may, by comparison, develop a less idealizing culture, one that celebrates differences among family members and contributions large and small. These groups tend to be more accepting, and less likely to make broad judgments based on specific differences. In reality, both dynamics are important and mutually reinforcing: unconditional acceptance and conditional acceptance (that is, the idea that it is OK to encourage an individual to modify behavior that is not ideal for a group). These are two sides of a paradox. Underlying a healthy business family's approach to family is unconditional acceptance, but part of their success in business is conditional acceptance – of people, ideas, and processes important to the business (as discussed in Chapter 1). A curious family business will be more likely to manage this paradox well (as well as other paradoxes), as they are less likely to make premature judgments about what is ultimately acceptable.

### *Cultural condition 2: Long-term perspective*

A central theme implicit in the approaches emphasized in this book is that of patience, or stepping back and taking the time necessary to understand and manage the paradox at hand. As Bonner Construction understands well, sometimes the best way to go fast is to slow down. Not surprisingly, then, cultures that emphasize speed, results, and outcomes without a balancing emphasis upon data gathering, investigation, and deliberation will have trouble managing paradoxes. Earlier we noted that Toyota encourages contradictory viewpoints, and challenges employees to find solutions by transcending differences rather than resorting to compromises. This kind of approach takes time. Integration and Synthesis also take time and effort. However, they lead to greater overall speed and quality of action in the long run than can be achieved otherwise.

Family businesses have some advantages regarding this cultural attribute. Their emphasis on continuity – keeping the family going for future generations – helps them maintain a long-term focus. Moreover, unlike widely held companies, family-controlled enterprises have the luxury of measuring results over decades, not quarters. This can give them the breathing room necessary for successful paradox management. Family businesses also tend to be more comfortable with incremental, rather than revolutionary, change. Instead of drastic pronouncements that take the business in a brand new direction, family firms typically invest the time needed to build understanding and consensus among stakeholders before making a decision. For them, it's about evolution, not revolution. This has its upsides and downsides that must be managed, however. A firm's continuity can be jeopardized by an over-emphasis on the long term, which can yield an absence of decisive action to drive short-term changes or benefits.

### *Cultural condition 3: World-class problem solving*

As illustrated throughout this book, paradoxes represent a unique kind of problem. Logically, family and business cultures that manage paradoxes well are ones that manage all kinds of problems capably. An attitude of continuous improvement is crucial, including the expectation that excellence is worth pursuing, along with a humble acceptance that there is always room for growth.

So how can family businesses foster a culture that includes world-class problem-solving skills? Model environments provide regular training opportunities for family members and employees, allowing them to build and apply their problem-solving skills. In fact, an emphasis on education pervades these cultures, with both the company and the family emphasizing educational planning and delivery.

An ample education budget is provided for these purposes – possibly as part of the shareholder relations or family council budgets. Well-developed vehicles exist for sharing learning among participants. These may be as simple as an email listserv, or as complicated as a family intranet or "learning conference." Learning partnerships may be developed with local colleges and universities. There are problem-solving task forces or committees, in both the business *and* the family. Individuals have well-developed teamwork and collaboration skills – and teams recruit for a variety of backgrounds, skills, and styles, knowing that this diversity will be important to their success. A multitude of evaluation and feedback methodologies are in place. These approaches go well beyond simple performance appraisals. There is an expectation that systems and processes, in the family and the business, will be evaluated or audited regularly. Updates and reports of continuous improvement measures are published regularly to a wide audience.

These components provide employees and family members with

multiple fora and channels for questioning "business as usual" – in fact, in these cultures, business as usual is a focus on continuous improvement. The resultant culture strongly supports both Either/Or *and* Both/*AND* approaches. Again, family businesses' focus on continuity helps: sustainable, genuine improvement usually takes time, making family businesses perfect incubators for cultures that emphasize, and are more likely to foster, world-class problem solving.

***Cultural capability 4: Solid trust***

Managing paradoxes well requires a culture of trust within the family and business. This gives family businesses an advantage over others, because family firms report that trust, along with integrity, is their most common value. So what are the key features of a culture of trust?

- ❑ Sincere curiosity, respect and honor for differing points of view, because trust is built through genuine listening and learning.
- ❑ The presence of vulnerability, because trust flourishes when individuals are willing to become mutually dependent in significant ways.
- ❑ Well-developed communication and conflict-management skills, because understanding others is not always easy, especially when others hold views different from our own.
- ❑ Agreed-upon frameworks within which fair process can take place in a reliable manner, because trust relies upon clarity and consistency.
- ❑ Long-term perspective, because trust is built through reliable, consistent behavior over a significant period of time.

Do family businesses tend to have higher levels of trust than widely held companies? While there is no clear answer, most families in business recognize that trust is one of the most essential conditions for successful continuity. Consequently, they actively seek to strengthen trust. For example, family meetings and other gatherings are organized as deliberate opportunities for individuals to get to know each other better and build stronger, more trusting relationships. Those family businesses that actively pursue the development of trust will typically have more trust-rich cultures.

However, many of the factors that promote trust can also threaten it.

A family's long history together can present multiple tests of trust. For example, in many family businesses, one family branch may hold on to resentment or suspicion of other family branches based on traumatic conflicts that occurred many years ago. In some cases, family descendants don't even know the exact source of their feud; they know only to keep it going.

These low-trust cultures are not friendly to the Both/*AND* way of thinking, and thus, struggle with paradox management. But other, more trust-laden cultures foster productive paradox management in part because members are comfortable with uncertainty and ambiguity, because they know they can rely on the group to manage through new and difficult problems. Success in this regard helps imbue the culture with even more trust.

### *Cultural capability 5: Extensive communication*

Another key cultural contributor to a family's and a business' ability to effectively manage paradoxes is communication. Communication is integral to success in most endeavors; but it is particularly important to managing paradox. The ability to identify the paradox in play and then develop an approach for its ongoing management requires effective dialogue among all involved.

As has been discussed, paradoxes bring together two truths that might appear to be opposing. Often, those involved have two different points of view about one side or the other. This is where communication comes in. In order to move past personal feelings about one side of the paradox or the other, it is critical to discuss the key opportunities and weaknesses of each side, and to do so in a respectful and curiously critical way. (The Polarity Map™ is a tool that is helpful in this regard.) This requires those involved to be open in their stance toward one another, and to focus on breaking any deadlocks by finding points of agreement within key issues and, ultimately, a win–win outcome.

Firms that are particularly good at open, active communication have developed fora for this type of communication. Some meetings are meant for reporting and are more informational, while others are meant to bring out issues and determine whether further attention should be given to a specific issue, and if so, who should take the lead. This approach may well be formalized as a specific part of a task force process employed in a company.

Communication is an area that is difficult for many groups and individuals, so it is not surprising that many firms, both public and private, struggle to make and keep it part of daily routine. Family businesses, in particular, are often conflict-averse. Some of this is actually rooted in their long-term focus, because they know they will see each other and be together frequently, both inside and outside the business. So, in the domain of paradoxes, especially some of the most difficult ones that emerge through conflicts within the business system or generational transitions, it is vital to establish a process (such as regular check-in sessions or retreats) to welcome these difficult conversations in a non-confrontational, less personal way.

With an active focus on developing these five cultural elements – including a willingness to learn from mistakes – families can foster an environment highly conducive to successful paradox management.

## FROM IMPLICIT TO EXPLICIT

Although many family businesses develop the ability to recognize and manage paradoxes, this capacity is largely instinctive rather than deliberate. However, as firms survive and thrive across the decades, they have the opportunity to evolve into Enterprising Families, and this implicit ability becomes more explicit. Several model family firms – Beretta and Cargill, among them – have made paradox management a cornerstone of their strategic approaches.

A central purpose of this book has been to make the natural abilities demonstrated by successful Enterprising Families more explicit. As family firms become more aware of the paradoxes in their families and business, they can apply the tools and techniques provided in this book more deliberately. This final section will present several ways to help you make implicit paradox management more explicit.

Recall the Family-First, Business-First Assessment introduced just prior to Chapter 1 (on p. 18). If you filled out the survey, you began the process of making your implicit knowledge more explicit. The survey can reveal your preferences regarding a business-first or family-first orientation. It will help you more consciously approach specific family business issues that may be layered in paradoxes. First, the awareness will help you understand your own viewpoint and biases and, in turn, the preferences of others. Armed with this deeper understanding on the part of individuals, the family business will be better able to identify and manage paradoxes.

A more explicit understanding of paradoxes also exists in the areas of generational transitions and conflicts resulting from family–management–ownership interactions. Understanding the genesis of these paradoxes is very helpful – whether you have already faced and conquered them, are currently living with them, or see them on the horizon. Families can place themselves within the generational oscillation model presented in Chapter 3 and/or anticipate tensions that may arise at the intersections of family, management, and ownership discussed in Chapter 4. The paradoxes discussed in Chapters 3 and 4 might be thought of as the "classics" for family business, and are compiled in Figure 7.1. These classics, combined with the frameworks and tools presented in Part III, provide a powerful base from which family businesses can operate.

Finally, using the paradox management continuum and the Polarity Map™ can also help groups move from implicit to explicit management of paradox. Making sure that these frameworks are well known among key members of the organization can go a long way towards instilling the capacity and capability for paradox management. Teaching the continuum and map is especially important as generational transitions unfold and natural tension points arise.

## A LOOK TOWARD FUSION

The more time and effort a family business spends exploring and understanding the many paradoxes it faces, the more capable it will become in recognizing and managing future paradoxes. Paradox management can become as natural as breathing as it moves from an implicit to more of an explicit process. Those most experienced in harnessing paradox will model best practices for others. This will help groups and individuals organization-wide move quickly from feeling frustrated by contradiction-riddled problems to calmly addressing the issues and even to look forward to paradox management.

Family businesses that hone their paradox management skills will find it easier to reach the levels of Integration, Synthesis, and Fusion

| CLASSIC FAMILY BUSINESS PARADOXES | | | | | |
|---|---|---|---|---|---|
| GENERATIONAL TRANSITION SHIFTS | | | FAMILY BUSINESS SYSTEM CONFLICTS | | |
| FOUNDER | SIBLING PARTNERSHIP | COUSIN COLLABORATIVE | FAMILY-MANAGEMENT | MANAGEMENT-OWNERSHIP | OWNERSHIP-FAMILY |
| ROOTS & WINGS | WORK & HOME | LOYALTY & FREEDOM | INCLUSIVE & SELECTIVE | REPRESENTATION & QUALIFICTIONS | EQUITY & MERIT |
| ACTION & PLANNING | OPPORTUNISTIC & CORE | INVEST & HARVEST | MARKET & NEEDS | HARVEST & INVEST | WORK & FUN |
| EXPEDIENCE & PATIENCE | TASK & PROCESS | PRIVACY & TRANSPARENCY | | | |
| CONTROL & TRUST | INDIVIDUAL & COLLECTIVE | FORMAL & INFORMAL | | | |
| PROPRIETORSHIP & STEWARDSHIP | MERIT & EQUALITY | ONE FAMILY & INDIVIDUAL BRANCH | | | |

**Figure 7.1** *Classic family business paradoxes*

with paradoxes. Over time, the two seemingly opposing sides of the paradox will merge naturally. For example, the following Synthesis statements may evolve from the paradoxes noted in Table 7.2.

**Table 7.2** *Paradoxes and Synthesis statements*

| **Paradox** | **Example Synthesis statements** |
|---|---|
| Tradition *and* change | True preservation of our traditions requires constant change, and productive change must be grounded in a foundation of tradition. |
| Individual *and* collective | Actions that strengthen the individual will automatically strengthen the collective, and actions that strengthen the collective automatically strengthen the individual. |
| Candor *and* diplomacy | In order to provide information or feedback effectively, we must be able to be honestly diplomatic and diplomatically honest. |

The overarching Synthesis, then, is the Enterprising Family – which, at its core, represents a healthy expression of both family *and* business. As the business grows stronger, the family is naturally strengthened as well. As family bonds improve, the business also becomes more capable. The relationship between the two is not one of competition for scarce resources, but one of Fusion. The interests of one become indistinguishable from those of the other – what strengthens the family can only bolster the business, and the continued success of the business means greater harmony for the family. That's what the ongoing pursuit of paradox management, as part of a family business's quest for continuous improvement, can yield.

# Appendices

*This page intentionally left blank*

# Appendix A

# Historical Perspective on Paradox[1]

Paradoxes have always existed; they are a part of life. Yet they are very intriguing parts of life: philosophers, writers, and thinkers of every ilk have long sought to understand our world by probing the paradoxical cruxes around us. Though often confusing or frustrating, most paradoxes feature a level of complexity that typically holds some kind of truth. Many thinkers, then, not only examined specific paradoxes and the general phenomenon they represent, but also built complicated systems of thought that incorporated paradoxes. Some of these worldviews are fundamental to Western thought, society, and culture.

The work of diverse thinkers like Hegel, Kant, Shakespeare, Bohr, and Einstein, among others, suggests that a paradox is not something to be afraid of, but something to be embraced, understood, and ultimately wielded as a tool to promote progress. What follows is an examination of how paradox has been treated in a number of domains over many centuries of thought.

## HEGEL'S DIALECTIC: MACRO-HISTORY AS PARADOX[2]

Georg Wilhelm Friedrich Hegel is held as one of the most important philosophers in modern Western thought. Hegelian dialectic had strong influence, most famously on Karl Marx, who relied on it to construct his communist worldview. Hegel's breakdown of history as a dialectical process is also an ideal example of the movement of paradoxes through history.

What is a dialectic? Generally speaking, a dialectic refers to a process that seeks to discover a truth by exploring opposing or paradoxical forces. For example, the Greeks utilized a dialectic approach in Socratic dialogue. Socrates believed the most effective way to uncover truth involved a system of probing questions – a dialogue – between people, a process that challenged the validity of every logical step discussed.

In fact, Hegel, saw history a bit like Socrates saw dialogue. History to Hegel is a systemic process of dialectics. How did the dialectics evolve? First, an idea, phenomenon, movement, or circumstance develops within the course of history. This idea becomes a *thesis*. But with time, an opposing idea, phenomenon, movement, or circumstance inevitably arises. This is the *antithesis*. The thesis and antithesis may go through a protracted time of opposition, or they may not. Regardless, as history churns forward, their differences are resolved to form a *synthesis*. The synthesis may arise as the result of a war, a natural disaster, a social or political shift, or simply the passage of time. However it emerges, the synthesis becomes its own idea, phenomenon, movement, or circumstance – that is, the synthesis becomes a new thesis, destined to be opposed by a new antithesis, and so on.

Take, for example, the French Revolution. For centuries, France was ruled by an oppressively autocratic monarchy. In dialectic terms, that's the thesis. The antithesis, then, is the intellectual enlightenment pushed by Voltaire and others in the early eighteenth century. The enlightenment introduced the then-radical concepts of suffrage and enfranchisement of *all* citizens (or at least, white male citizens).

Although there are hundreds of theories for what exactly caused the French Revolution, if we take a macro-view of the French Revolution as a historical movement, it's easy to see it as the precise moment of conflict between the two theses. Yet the resulting synthesis could not be considered a victory of democracy. Because the synthesis is actually a higher-order combination of both thesis *and* antithesis, it couldn't be represented by either side's trumping the other. And Napoleon's brutal rule was not exactly what the monarchists or the leaders of the enlightenment had in mind.

It's important to remember, then, that Hegel's notion of a historical synthesis combines the two theses. The synthesis of black and white isn't gray – it's a new system of optics that allows for a dual and concurrent perception of both black *and* white.

## KANT'S SEMINAL PARADOXES[3]

Philosophy of history is by no means the only branch of philosophy in which paradox is central. Immanuel Kant is well known for his paradoxical theories on everything from art to morality to international relations to epistemology.

His seminal theories on how to judge art, for example, contain three major paradoxes. First, Kant says that in order to judge art we must be disinterested. That is, Kant says that in order to appreciate art fully, we must focus attention not on the object or concept of the piece but on its effect on the perceiver. In this way, a pacifist can more objectively consider the power of an artwork representing a gun, for example.

The paradoxes in Kant's aesthetics go even deeper. Kant believes that art must not have a purpose, yet champions a view that appraises beauty based on the "purposiveness" of a work. Purposiveness can be thought of as the technical and intellectual intentionality of a work of art. The purposiveness of a painting, for example, is the arrangement of brush strokes on a canvas, as well as use of light, perspective, composition, and the like.

Related to this notion is Kant's argument for subjective universality, a paradox in itself. To Kant, purpose implicates emotions and desires, and interferes with the judgment of taste because an individual's emotions are obviously not universal. Kant wants aesthetic beauty to be universally recognizable, through (disinterested) taste, but insofar as it is based on subjects' satisfaction and even though every subject's satisfaction is different, such beauty must be able to be discerned by any/every subject. (Kant titles a section in his *Critique* "The pure judgment of taste is indifferent of charm and emotion.") Kant here recalls purposiveness as one of the key links in being able to judge beauty. Everyone is able to recognize brilliant purposiveness, as in the universally acclaimed technique Rembrandt used in painting with so many layers of paint.

Kant's famous moral theory, the categorical imperative, is also laced with paradox. To decide if an action is moral, Kant says, we must propose a maxim for ourselves that can be applied to everyone. Like the categorical imperative, the transcendental formula of public right begins with the formulation of a maxim, and like the categorical imperative, it then undergoes a test to examine whether or not it can be universally ("categorically") applied. In the case of the transcendental formula of public right, the test involves asking whether this maxim can be made public without, as Kant says, "at the same time defeating my own intention." In other words, if presenting it to the public rendered it unpopular, then the maxim is by definition unfeasible. Thus, in order to put this rather idealistic principle into practice, we must conceive innumerable maxims in order to find ones that the public – often fickle and capricious – would find suitable.

Kant also sounds off on whether morality is different in public or private. In order to be moral, for example, we must not lie. But what if someone is a public official with private information relating to their nation's security? If a journalist asks such an individual to confirm such information, should they lie? Kant believes that his categorical imperative and transcendental formula of public right are universal, and thus apply in all social situations, including the political realm. Kant says, "If we find it absolutely necessary to couple politics with the concept of right … the compatibility of the two must be conceded." So Kant envisions a "moral politician:" that is, one who guides politics based on guidelines of morality. But because his moral universalism expects morality to apply to the political realm, Kant cannot envision a "political moralist," who contrives morals "to suit the statesman's advantage."[4]

## REALISM AND IDEALISM IN INTERNATIONAL RELATIONS

The field of international relations is filled with paradoxes even beyond Kant's morals. Perhaps the largest is the dual necessities of realism and idealism.

Realism is a system of policies based on self-protection. It assumes that other players are not to be trusted, that a nation should avoid placing itself in even a *potentially* vulnerable situation. In other words, realism holds that the security of one nation is the paramount priority. No other policy item should be implemented at the cost of security. One of the earliest examples of realism is Sun Tzu's sixth-century *The Art of War*. The concisely phrased little book served as the foundation for much of Eastern military strategy, and is still cited today for its many aphorisms applicable to every sphere of life. In more modern times, thinkers like Niccolo Machiavelli – who said the best way to govern was through fear – and George F. Kennan – who advocated containment of Soviet Russia through the twentieth century – helped shape intellectual approaches to international relations from the point of view of pragmatic, real threats to the nation. It's no wonder realism is often referred to as "power politics."

On the other hand is idealism in international relations, a school of thought that prioritizes internal policy in a way that allows for a firm domestic base from which to build international influence? President Woodrow Wilson is perhaps the most famous proponent of international idealism. Even though he failed, in the end, to overcome isolationism after the First World War, his speeches and work with the League of Nations and Congress left a lasting impression.

Today, neoconservatives stand as a sort of Hegelian synthesis in the paradoxical relationship between idealism and realism. Although neoconservatives believe in promoting "ideal" conditions, they believe in establishing those conditions internationally, often using very "realist" approaches tied into security and power.

The fact is, every state operates using both realist *and* idealist goals and methods. It is often the states that thrive within the two opposing concepts that stand above the rest. So how do we reconcile the paradox? It must be managed without relying too heavily on either realism or idealism individually. Part of the reason for the United States becoming the most globally influential nation was how the country has handled this paradox.

## THE TWENTIETH-CENTURY UNITED STATES AS THE ULTIMATE PARADOX[5]

Some see the United States as a paragon of paradox. Paradoxes throughout the history of the United States have helped define it for ardent patriots and vocal dissidents alike. It speaks as the freest country in the world, and yet has a history marred by large-scale, systemic cruelty.

Glen Jeansonne, in his book *A Time of Paradox*, argues that the twentieth-century United States was paradox personified. It was a time when technology advanced our living standards, and also brought humanity face to face with new terrorizing ways to be killed en masse. The United States dropped two atomic bombs, developed hydrogen bombs with the capability to set fire to the entire global atmosphere, and yet made drastic medical advances and landed humans on the moon for the first time.

The very political basis in the United States is paradoxical. The democratic republic crafted by the founding fathers is ideally a sort of synthesis between the oppressive monarchy they had thrown off and all-out democracy, which they feared because of its potential for decentralized chaos and rule by the masses. Three branches of government were formed instead, each with certain limited powers. In other words, centralization was achieved with a decentralized central power. In general, with its houses split into elite (Senate) and common (House of Representatives), with representatives who vote on each issue independent of every constituent's wish, the bifurcated democratic republic is deeply paradoxical.

## SCIENTIFIC PARADOXES FROM QUANTUM PHYSICS TO EPISTEMOLOGY

If the twentieth century was so different from previous centuries because of the exponential development and impact of technology, then it makes sense that we would find paradoxes in this domain, too.

Albert Einstein's profound discoveries in quantum physics may have (quite literally) shaken the world, but they were not without opposition. A younger school of scientists led by Niels Bohr soon emerged to challenge their predecessors, and a classic generational battle ensued.[6] The paradox between the two schools of thought is not just that they disagreed with each other over their analyses of mathematical, physical, theoretical, and approaches to evidence. Rather, the paradox is based in their divergent ways of approaching the evidence to begin with. So, according to Sandro Petrucciolo's book *Atoms, Metaphors and Paradoxes*, Einstein could argue for a programmatic approach, which involved complete descriptions via the mathematic probability of a situation, irrespective of anything actually observed, and Bohr could argue for the opposite, the Copenhagen approach, which involved drawing conclusions based on what is observable, even if only theoretically.

Debating the value of observation is not a twentieth-century phenomenon related strictly to technology. In the older scientific field of epistemology, technology has only recently contributed to an ancient philosophic tradition. Naturally, Kant's paradoxical way of thinking also applied here. How do we know what we know? Along with religion and morality, epistemology is probably the most discussed field of philosophy, and yet recently philosophers have been replaced by neuroscientists and technology tracing how knowledge is processed in the human brain.

But before technology entered the conversation, thinkers tried to answer this tricky question, usually falling on one side of a long-standing argument between John Locke's concept of *tabula rasa* – the blank slate – and Rene Descartes' idea of *ergo cogito sum*. Locke believed that humans were born a blank slate, onto which experiences (via the senses) etch the knowledge carried through life. Descartes, on the other hand, put no trust in humans' senses, arguing that the only way we could know anything was by asking questions – in other words, using the ability to think. Hence the notion of "I think, therefore I am." That led to a dualistic understanding of the body and the mind as two separate entities.

Kant falls somewhere in the middle, as might be expected. His theory is that while experiences influence knowledge, humans are born with certain categories within the mind in which our knowledge is formed. Modern technological approaches to the mind are generally aligned with this idea: it is the classic nature/nurture debate – a paradox, too.

## SHAKESPEARE'S PARADOX

Paradox has a well-established place in literature, especially in the classics, which often focus on timeless, universal aspects of life. Consider Shakespeare. His plays often bring out some sort of universal truth that still holds value centuries later. For example, a book interpreting Shakespeare's play *The Merchant of Venice* illuminates the paradox of justice *and* mercy:

> Our investigation of the nature of bonds has raised a fundamental paradox, the need for the coexistence of mercy and justice. The task of this chapter is

> not to choose one at the expense of the other, nor to demonstrate that there is no real contradiction between them. It would be entirely against the spirit of Shakespeare to do either. What Shakespeare does in *The Merchant of Venice* is to accept the necessity and the mutual contradiction of mercy and justice, and to generate a dramatic world out of their continued struggle. As he develops a poetic vocabulary of metaphors and puns and plot twists and historical and mythological allusions to embody the struggle, the legal paradox of mercy and justice opens into wider and wider fields of relevance: morality, economics, physics, human physiology and evolution, religious history, theology, linguistics, aesthetics, cosmology. The point is not so much to resolve the paradox of mercy and justice, as it is to trace Shakespeare's own demonstration of how the paradox constructs the world. The solution to its puzzles is not a neat one that would dispose of the problem once and for all, but rather the continuation of the struggle itself.[7]

In that passage, several words and phrases, listed below, embody the feeling and meaning of paradoxes. These "truths," if you will, can be viewed as elements of a framework to keep in mind when identifying and managing paradoxes. Many of them are echoed in the business-book excerpts in Appendix B.

- ❑ coexistence
- ❑ not to choose one at the expense of the other
- ❑ accept the necessity and the mutual contradiction
- ❑ struggle
- ❑ point is not so much to resolve
- ❑ solution to its puzzles is not a neat one that would dispose of the problem once and for all
- ❑ continuation of the confrontational paradigm.

Moreover, the paradox of justice and mercy is one that nearly anyone involved in a family business can relate to. Each family member has interests, opportunities, and capabilities that may or may not be used in some way to benefit the family or the business. What happens in the family business system when something goes wrong for one of its members, either by their own doing, or by a circumstance beyond their control? Is justice sought or mercy administered? To us the answer must be to seek both, for one without the other will only feed the next problem or conflict within the family business system.

## PARADOXES IN TRADITIONAL EASTERN THOUGHT

His Holiness the Dalai Lama is today's most visible and outspoken representative of Buddhism, and his lectures, writings, and thoughts on applying Buddhism to contemporary times are the best place to begin a quest to understand the paradoxes in Buddhism.[8] A good starting point is the Dalai Lama's worldview: "The basic fact is that all sentient beings, particularly human beings, want happiness and do not want to suffer."

That idea sounds simple, but it's rife with complexity. For example, what if short-term happiness leads to long-term pain? The short term versus the long term is a universal paradox, and it's one that applies to many spheres of life, including family business. The Dalai Lama says that in the case where short-term and long-term interests and consequences are contradictory, we should keep the long-term interest as the top priority. That means that even if the short-term option involves pain and suffering – his terms – it is worth persevering if the long-term option will bring happiness. This is likely an approach followed by many family businesses.

Buddhism offers many other complications. For example, there are different types of short-term/long-term paths. There are internal and external paths, conceptual and experiential paths, and abstract and tangible paths. If the quest for supreme happiness at both internal and external levels seems too large a paradox to handle, especially while simultaneously trying to balance short and long-term interests, the Dalai Lama agrees. He returns to the Buddhist dharma, and lists what the Buddha called "basic human good qualities." These qualities, according to the Dalai Lama, are fundamentally "spiritual." They are not religious, he is careful to point out, but rather universal qualities every human is born with. They are:

- human affection
- a sense of involvement
- honesty
- discipline
- human intelligence properly guided by motivation.

These basic human qualities make humans good, and all humans are born good. But as simple as that may sound at first, it is in fact a tremendously sophisticated – and paradoxical – tenet of Buddhist thought. Because though all may be born with these qualities, human experience is not universal; paths, forms of suffering, and ways of experiencing happiness diverge. The Dalai Lama says, "Buddhists usually say that there is no absolute and that everything is relative." Another Buddhist paradox, then, is between universal *and* relative.

Another paradox of focus for the Dalai Lama involves the human brain: everyone has a brain, but each one is different. According to the Dalai Lama, "The wonderful human brain is the source of our strength and the source of our future … if we use the brilliant human mind the wrong way, it is really a disaster." He focuses on the universality of the brain's *potential.* Humans' immense potential girds the Dalai Lama's belief that humans are the most powerful species on earth. That's why he calls it "human potential."

Utilizing the brain to maximize human potential is the best route to happiness. Yet, in order to succeed in this effort, we must manage another Buddhist paradox: that between self-confidence *and* egotism. The Dalai Lama says there is no way to reach our human potential without human confidence, but warns that an excess of self-confidence fosters narcissism and selfishness. Still, he is entirely optimistic that each human can find a unique path to happiness. Part of the support for this belief is the power of nature, which helps humans navigate various paradoxes. The Dalai Lama says:

> It is my belief that the human brain and basic human compassion are by nature in some kind of balance. Sometimes, when we grow up, we may neglect human affection and simply concentrate on the human brain, thus losing the balance. It is then that disasters and unwelcome things happen. If we look at different species of mammals, we will see that nature is very important and that it is a forceful factor that creates some sort of balanced way.

Paradoxes mitigated by balance are also prominent in Taoism, another ancient Eastern philosophy. The *Tao Te Ching* (roughly translated as "Classic of the Way and Virtue") is a series of musings Lao Tzu wrote some 2,500 years ago. But Lao Tzu did not want them to be ultimate moral directives like the Ten Commandments. The *Tao* is meant to be appropriated, translated, and understood independently by each generation – indeed, by each person.

It's true that most religious texts share the paradox of a solid unchanging text that flexibly accommodates each individual's interpretation, and thus changes for each reader; but this notion is even more powerful for the *Tao*. In fact, the *Tao* is taught as strictly experiential and not at all conceptual. In other words, Taoists believe that the only way to live according to Lao Tzu's guidelines is to experience the *Tao* as thoroughly as possible, rather than merely considering it and ruminating on it. Thus, while "Tao" means God, creation, nature, Way of all Life, and universal essence and its manifestation, "Te" means action, virtue, morality, beauty, and gracious behavior. So, action and experience are core elements of Lao Tzu's guide.

Modern interpretations of the *Tao*, such as that of Mantak Chia and Tao Huang,[9] are quick to point out that the language in the *Tao* is purposively vague: it is up to the reader to understand the experiential context, to make the meditations personal. Chia and Huang say the *Tao* is "subtle and impossible to grasp with the conceptual mind," and that it's "inaccessible to normal thought, language, or perception." Other adjectives they use include "invisible," "unfathomable," "unreachable," "untraceable," and "beyond comprehension." They say, "To define the Tao is to listen to silence."

Elsewhere in this interpretation is the importance of communication. Communication is important not only because it is experiential, but because it takes us closer to our own true Tao. But external communication is different from – oppositional to, even – inner voice. Our inner voice helps us understand the true way of the *Tao*, even as the inner voice shifts constantly, too.

These paradoxes within Taoism are hardly the result of shoddy writing or lazy interpretation; they are held as making the *Tao* what it is: a profound and ancient approach to life that shifts along with life itself. Thus, what one might call vagueness in the *Tao*, another would call flexibility. It is the universal applicability of the *Tao* that has allowed it to persist across generations, just as any long-standing, thriving business will change and shift and transform with the times – as long, perhaps, as the "inner voice" is being heard, even when it's silent.

## CONCLUSION

It is clear that paradoxes have been and will continue to be found in almost every system of thought. That's partly because paradox is a lens through which to conceptualize and understand a dynamic or a problem. What Hegel, Kant, Einstein, the Dalai Lama, Lao Tzu, and others understand is that these paradoxes, or a view that embraces finding paradoxes, need not be feared. Quite the opposite: they must be probed, because within their complications lies a kernel of fresh perspective, the understanding of which can rapidly advance progress.

Thus in family business, those who seek out and conquer paradox will move forward.

# Appendix B

# Paradoxes in Business Literature

As Appendix A highlights, the discussion and study of paradoxes has been around for centuries. Thus, this book's aim is to bring to the surface, in very concrete terms, what a paradox is and how to manage paradoxes successfully. In this context, this Appendix provides a backdrop of the treatment of paradox in more recent business research and books, especially those that have illuminated paradox as integral to ongoing business success.

Keep a broad definition of paradox in mind when reading the material that follows – especially the business book excerpts – as the terms and phrases used to describe paradox-related phenomena may differ from author to author; yet the core concepts and messages are virtually identical. The breadth of paradox-related material presented here should help build appreciation of the potential impact of unrecognized and unmanaged paradoxes within family businesses.

## PARADOX IN CURRENT BUSINESS THINKING

Although the field of business management does not address paradox in the way it has addressed the general idea of problem solving, paradox management has emerged as an integral component for successful companies. In recent decades, business books have not only identified paradoxes, but have suggested that managing them is critical to companies' overall success. The list below, though not meant to be comprehensive, includes many of the more recent and/or highly visible business books that highlight paradoxes. This appendix considers several of these (greyed in the list below) in more detail in the analysis that follows.

*In Search of Excellence*, Thomas J. Peters and Robert H. Waterman, Jr. (1982)
*The Seven Habits of Highly Effective People*, Stephen R. Covey (1989)
*Polarity Management*, Barry Johnson (1992)
*The Paradox of Success*, John R. O'Neil (1993)
*Built to Last*, Jim Collins and Jerry I. Porras (1994)
*Paradoxical Thinking*, Jerry Fletcher and Kelle Olwyler (1997)
*Good to Great,* Jim Collins (2001)
*The Paradox of Excellence*, David Mosby and Michael Weissman (2005)
*The Three Tensions*, Dominic Dodd and Ken Favaro (2007)
*Profit or Growth*, Bala Chakravarthy and Peter Lorange (2007)
*Firms of Endearment*, Raj Sisodia, Jag Sheth, and David B. Wolfe (2007)
*How the Mighty Fall*, Jim Collins (2009)
*The Time Paradox*, Philip Zimbardo (2009)

## *Firms of Endearment*

The premise of *Firms of Endearment* is that many companies have thrived by maintaining strong passion and purpose – "This book is about gaining 'share of heart,' not just 'share of wallet,'" the inside jacket cover states. The companies profiled, referred to as Firms of Endearment (FoE), number 28 in total, of which 13 are privately held; eight of those are family companies. Of those that are public, many are strong family-based companies where the founding family is still strongly involved and/or still holds some level of ownership (such as Toyota, Johnson & Johnson, and Timberland). The book points out that compared with S&P returns, these (public) companies returned 1,026 percent for investors over a ten-year period ending June 2006.

How do these FoEs achieve this unbelievable return? According to the authors, they do it through these activities and perspectives:

- ❑ freely challenge industry dogma
- ❑ create value by aligning stakeholder interests

- ❑ are willing to break traditional trade-offs
- ❑ operate with a long-term perspective
- ❑ favor organic growth to growing by mergers and acquisitions
- ❑ blend work and play
- ❑ reject traditional marketing models.[1]

These characteristics overlap significantly with the idea of accepting paradoxes and managing them to benefit the company. The following *Firms of Endearment* excerpt, from the section on companies' willingness to break traditional trade-offs, supports this book's notion of Both/*AND* thinking, and how it can help managers accommodate seemingly contradictory items like high wages *and* high profits:

> Thinking in terms of tradeoffs is a mainstay in business. It derives from the disposition of the scientifically grounded Western mind to value "if/then" and "either/or" constructs over "both/and" constructs .... The alternative style of thinking – both/and – opens up the mind to accommodate seemingly contradictory conditions (for example, high wages/high profit margins) and avoids the limitations of tradeoff computations (for example, there is only one best way to accomplish something).

The book presents several examples of FoEs rejecting tradeoff thinking and embracing Both/*AND*:

- ❑ *Jet Blue*: Low prices *and* Higher-quality travel experience
- ❑ *Costco*: Uncommonly low mark-ups *and* High-quality products
- ❑ *Amazon*: Exceptional service *and* Low prices (often with free shipping)
- ❑ *Trader Joe's*: Inexpensive *and* Exotic food products.

One of the key paradoxes that FoEs seem to have figured out is how to provide excellent wages to their employees *and* value to the customers. There's not much of a secret to it: FoEs have found that the seemingly extra cost of paying employees well is offset by the higher productivity of their happier employees, who in turn deliver greater service to customers. Thus the company takes care of the employees by paying well, the employees take care of the customers by serving them better, and the customers take care of the employees (and the company) by coming back. The book explains this in detail:

> One tradeoff that FoEs consistently break is between employee wages and value to customers .... They offer outstanding wages to their employees and competitive prices to their customers – and make healthy profits to boot ... The greater productivity of higher-caliber employees and lower employee turnover in part explains this .... the link between satisfied employees and customer loyalty is beyond question .... FoEs in general do better in getting share of wallet by a far greater focus on share of heart than is customary in their industries.

The other point worth discussing is that FoEs favor organic growth, or a long-term perspective, similar to that of family businesses. For example, the book discusses how the eastern US grocery chain Wegmans opens only two or three new stores each year, despite receiving thousands of letters clamoring for more locations.

> Wegmans' priority is to ensure that each new store is a community event, employees are fully trained and that they have the capability to move their "best and brightest" around to each new location to ensure successful opening.

*Firms of Endearment* concludes with a paradox, although not called that specifically:

> They [FoEs] know that the most effective way to compete in today's business world is by operating in the open and adding to their core asset base the value that all stakeholders bring to the table. This then generates the augmented value that the company can leverage for the benefit of all.

The quote above is about working hand in hand with all stakeholders (society, employees, investors, customers, and partners) to create "value" that benefits all – not just the company. In turn, the FoEs reap the benefit from supporting all their stakeholders by continuing to grow the value of the company itself. Managing this paradox of company value *and* other stakeholder value has been the cornerstone of success for FoEs.

### *Profit or Growth*

In *Profit or Growth*, Bala Chakravarthy and Peter Lorange focus on a paradox that is often the undoing of many publicly listed companies:

attaining profits while not stifling growth. Because family firms can generally take a longer view, this paradox is less central.

*Profit or Growth*'s first chapter, "The performance dilemmas," highlights the tension between profitability *and* growth (a paradox) and goes on to discuss what underlies driving profitable growth (achieving Both/*AND*, effectively). The book cites how Gerard Kleisterlee, CEO of Royal Philips Electronics, addressed this and other paradoxes (which he calls "dilemmas"):

> For Kleisterlee, seeking profitability and growth meant investing in the core businesses of Philips and developing new businesses for the future, driving efficiency and nurturing innovation, and insisting on strict deliverables from each organizational silo even when encouraging them to share freely with each other. Underlying the performance dilemma then was a cluster of other dilemmas that needed to be managed.
>
> Unlike when making decisions, no alternative can be discarded when managing dilemmas. Instead, the two alternatives need to be balanced continuously. This is the balancing act that managers must learn to master if they are to sustain profitable growth. As Kleisterlee puts it, managing dilemmas is the essence of managerial work.[2]

In general, *Profit or Growth* contains many parallels to the treatment of paradox in this book. For example, Kleisterlee's "dilemma" is synonymous with "paradox" in this book. Second, notice that "underneath" the CEO's paradox of focus (profitability and growth) are several others (highlighted by the underlining in the excerpt). Finally, he emphasizes the need to manage both sides of the dilemma or paradox to achieve the ultimate goal of profitable growth. Thus Kleisterlee's dilemmas have the same characteristics as this book's paradoxes: two opposing values, which on the surface appear to conflict, but upon further investigation, are mutually supportive and must be managed together.

In this example, attaining profitability and growth (in other words, managing the central paradox of profitability and growth) requires managing three associated paradoxes (underlined above): "the core *and* new business," "efficiency *and* innovation," and "strict deliverables from silos *and* sharing with others." That's a central idea in this book: paradoxes underlying paradoxes – for success, all must be managed.

The last paragraph is reminiscent of the present book's first chapter, as it distinguishes between a decision to be made and a paradox to be managed. Kleisterlee uses the term "balance," which is not about choosing one side of the issue and then the other, but rather mastering the management of both sides for the benefit, in the Philips case, of ultimately managing the central paradox, profit *and* growth.

Chapter 7 of *Profit or Growth*, "Directing renewal," includes two sections that speak directly to paradox – Continuity *and* Change and Managing Dilemmas.

> In driving renewal, top management seeks to balance the culture of change that continuous renewal brings with a sense of continuity …
>
> The organization needs to feel anchored in something; this something is what Jim Collins and Jerry Porras call the core purpose and core values of a firm.
>
> The continuity that core purpose and core values provide a firm is vital to its renewal.

At the heart of these statements is the need to have some sense of stability or tradition within the organization, especially during times of significant change. This stability is often in the form of the core values and traditions of the organization itself. Chakravarthy and Lorange cite two such "core" traditions at medical device maker Medtronic: the first is a medallion ceremony started in the early 1960s, in which the CEO meets each new employee personally and presents them with a bronze medallion inscribed with the company's mission; the second is the annual holiday party at the company's Minneapolis headquarters, in which several patients and their physicians are invited to "tell their story of how they were restored to lead a full life." These unscripted stories are then relayed to all Medtronic locations worldwide. The traditions allow Medtronic employees across the globe to bond and then use the energy created by this mutual bond to propel them toward the next Medtronic innovation. Thus, this paradox of tradition *and* change is central to Medtronic's success in managing the paradox of growth *and* profit.

Due to their longer-term perspective, family businesses struggle less with the growth *and* profit paradox than pulic firms, for example; but it's still helpful to understand the paradox and how managing it plays a key role in business success.

### *The Three Tensions*

This book by Dominic Dodd and Ken Favaro focuses on three specific paradoxes, or tensions:

- profitability *and* growth
- whole *and* parts
- short term *and* long term.

Dodd and Favaro begin by stating that great performance rises above compromise. They continue by asserting that the tension created between each of these seemingly opposing objectives is what ultimately allows businesses to achieve both:

> there is a common bond: a necessary ingredient for the two objectives to act as complements rather than substitutes. If this bond is absent, the two objectives become substitutes: good performance on one will lead to poor performance on another. But if the bond is strong, then good and mutually reinforcing performance on both objectives is possible.[3]

The book asserts that each of the three central tensions has a unique bond (really a synthesis). *Customer benefit* is the bond between profitability *and* growth; *sustainable earnings* is the bond between short *and* long-term performance; and *diagonal assets* (resources and capabilities) is the bond between the whole *and* the parts of a company. They assert that managing these bonds, creating a synthesis, without compromise leads a company to superior performance.

Finally, Dodd and Favaro caution that when one tension is given preference or priority it leads to what is termed "the corporate cycle" – a self-defeating spiral of behavior that limits company performance. They suggest there has been little written about how to break this cycle:

> Although achieving many apparently conflicting objectives at the same time is central to the challenge of management, it is not yet central to the literature on management… there are many techniques for how to improve company performance on one objective that are silent on how to do so for the other. It is this one-sidedness that permits – even encourages – fashion in management.

The present book's Chapter 5 focuses on the need to further develop the discipline of management in this regard. Dodd and Favaro go on to discuss the need for new insights to this end:

> the need for a deeper understanding of how existing tools – standards, strategy, structure, process and culture – are best combined. The problem with many management innovations is not that they are intrinsically unhelpful to the search for good performance; the problem is that they are only effective as the company they keep – that is how they are deployed in combination. Much work is needed to produce new insights into how the many tools currently available to managers can be combined to help them perform well on the full combination of their performance objectives.

When investigating paradoxes, it is important that this process be understood in the broader context of problem-solving. Not every problem is a paradox to be managed. Problems encountered that are not paradoxes lend themselves to other sets of tools and processes. Thus, paradoxical management is not meant to replace the means by which organizations currently solve problems, but rather to enhance their problem-solving repertoire by providing additional tools and processes.

## *Good to Great*

*Good to Great* has sold over 2 million copies; this book, along with two others Jim Collins has written (or co-written), discussed next, has had great impact on the business world. For selected companies, the authors analyzed data over time, including defining actions and moments. As the book's name suggests, the goal was to identify components crucial to transforming a company from good to great. From this analysis a number of concepts emerged, including several related directly or indirectly to paradox management:

- ❑ Level 5 leadership
- ❑ Confront the brutal facts (yet never lose faith)
- ❑ A culture of discipline
- ❑ Technology accelerators.

Collins asserts that businesses are not capable of good-to-great transformations without the specific skills of Level 5 leadership.

> Level 5 leadership: Builds enduring greatness through a paradoxical blend of personal humility and professional will.[4]

It is important to understand the context of Level 5 leadership. Although Collins wished to avoid looking at executives' characteristics (seeing this as too easy an answer), his research team kept coming back to the fact that the executives in charge during a good-to-great transition were indeed unique. What was even more interesting is that the pattern displayed by these leaders "cuts against the grain of conventional wisdom, especially the belief that we need larger-than-life saviors with big personalities to transform companies." These leaders were indeed a "study in duality: modest *and* willful, humble *and* fearless." As an example of Level 5 leadership outside of the business world, Collins cites Abraham Lincoln. Collins says Lincoln was one of the few Level 5 presidents of the United States, one who would "never let his ego get in the way of his primary ambition for the larger cause of an enduring great nation."

Modest ← *AND* → Willful

Humble ← *AND* → Fearless

Another key concept from *Good to Great* also identified a paradox to be managed: Confront the brutal facts (yet never lose faith). Collins named this the Stockdale paradox (inspired by a former prisoner of war): "You must maintain unwavering faith that you can and will prevail in the end, regardless of the difficulties, AND at the same time have the discipline to confront the most brutal facts of the current reality, whatever they might be."

A culture of discipline, the third paradoxical component within Collins's book, is about managing the paradox that often is at the core of many family business issues, as mentioned earlier: tradition *and* change.

> A culture of discipline involves a duality. One the one hand, it requires people who adhere to a consistent system; yet, on the other hand, it give people freedom and responsibility within the framework of that system.

A final paradox-containing component in *Good to Great* is the use of

Technology accelerators: "[These companies] never use technology as the primary means of igniting a transformation, yet, paradoxically they are pioneers in the application of carefully selected technologies." It was noted that technology was never the cause for greatness or decline in those companies that achieved greatness, but rather "when used right, technology becomes an accelerator of momentum, not the creator of it."

Thus, each of the highlighted components within Collins's book has managing a specific paradox, or set of paradoxes, at its core, reinforcing how the need to understand and identify paradoxes, along with building capacity and capability to manage them, is crucial for business performance.

## *Built to Last* and *How the Mighty Fall*

*Built to Last*, written by Jim Collins (and Jerry Porras) before *Good to Great,* had a slightly different focus, but also included themes of paradox management as central to "visionary companies'" success. *Built to Last*'s goal was to identify comparable company pairs and tease out principles that made only one of them a visionary company. Visionary companies are defined as:

> premier institutions – crown jewels – in their industries, widely admired by their peers and having a long track record of making a significant impact on the world around them. The key point is that a visionary company is an organization – an institution ... visionary companies prosper over long periods of time, through multiple product life cycles and multiple generations of active leaders.[5]

In the introduction to the book's paperback edition, the authors highlight the need for continuity *and* change: "if there is any one 'secret' to an enduring great company, it is the ability to manage continuity and change – a discipline that must be consciously practiced, even by the most visionary companies." The book goes on to cite several companies, both previously included in the study as visionary and ones that are on the "radar screen" as potential additions. These included several that started as or continue to be family businesses: Hewlett-Packard, Johnson & Johnson, Walmart, Levi Strauss, and Cargill. The central idea is that these companies know what to keep sacred and what they can change – and act on this knowledge. Once again, the need to manage tradition *and* change.

*Built to Last* goes on to develop four key concepts, two of which are focused on managing paradoxes:

> Embrace the "Genius of the AND."
> Preserve the core/stimulate progress.

To Embrace the "Genius of the AND" is opposed to what is called the "Tyranny of the OR." Thus, we must become comfortable being uncomfortable. We must live with two seemingly contradictory forces or ideas at the same time, rather than succumbing to the Tyranny of the OR by choosing.

Instead of being oppressed by the Tyranny of the OR, highly visionary companies liberate themselves with the Genius of the AND – the ability to embrace both extremes of a number of dimensions at the same time. Instead of choosing between A OR B, they figure out how to have both A AND B. Figure B-1 highlights some of the paradoxes – apparent contradictions – in the visionary companies noted in *Built to Last*. Those highlighted are consistent with paradoxes that often thrive in family businesses in particular, and are discussed in more detail throughout this book.

| | *AND* | |
|---|---|---|
| investment for the long term | ⟷ | demands for short-term performance |
| clear vision/sense of direction | ⟷ | opportunism and experimentation |
| organization aligned with core ideology | ⟷ | organization adapted to its environment |

**Figure B-1** *Paradoxes in many of the visionary companies noted in* Built to Last

Note that the focus is not on "balancing" either side of the paradox, but rather on proactively seeking both sides. Balance implies going to the midpoint, fifty-fifty, half and half …. In short, a highly visionary company doesn't want to blend … it aims to … distinctly manage … both at the same time, all the time …. Irrational? Perhaps. Rare? Yes. Difficult? Absolutely. That's exactly what Enterprising Families must achieve, as discussed in the present book.

*Built to Last* highlights another paradox requiring thoughtful management: Preserve the core/stimulate progress, or stated another way, tradition *and* change:

> The interplay between core and progress is one of the most important findings from our work. In the spirit of the Genius of the AND, a visionary company does not seek mere balance between core and progress; it seeks to be both highly ideological and highly progressive at the same time, all the time. Indeed, core ideology and the drive for progress exist together in a visionary company … each element enables, complements and reinforces the other:
>
> - The core ideology enables the progress by providing a base of continuity around which a visionary company can evolve, experiment and change. By being clear about what is core (and therefore relatively fixed) a company can more easily seek variation and movement in all that is not core.
> - The drive to progress enables the core ideology, for without continual change and forward movement, the company – the carrier of the core – will fall behind in an ever-changing world and cease to be strong, or perhaps even to exist.

The authors go on to argue that:

> A highly visionary company does not simply have some vague set of intentions or passionate zeal around core and progress. To be sure, a highly visionary company does have these, but it also has concrete, tangible mechanisms to preserve the core ideology and stimulate progress.

The book cites several very concrete ways some of the visionary companies preserve the core: creating company universities and requiring every single employee to attend, instituting rigorous promote-from-within policies, creating a cult of service reinforced by tangible rewards and penalties, to name a few. These fit well into the present book's handling of the paradox of tradition *and* change.

*Built to Last* touts the notion of understanding and managing paradoxes and making them concrete so that they live in the organization. The present book builds on this by teaching family business members how to identify specific paradoxes in a given situation and then use processes and tools to develop a plan to ensure the tension created by the paradox is used to both bond the family *and* propel the business.

Note that some of these *Built to Last* companies have fallen from grace in recent years, as detailed in Collin's latest book, *How the Mighty Fall*. He suggests that one reason for failure is the hubris born of success, especially in regard to "Confusing the what and why." *How the Mighty Fall* states:

> Like an artist who pursues both enduring excellence and shocking creativity, great companies foster a productive tension between continuity and change. On the one hand, they adhere to the principles that produced success in the first place, yet on the other hand; they continually evolve, modifying their approach with creative improvements and intelligent adaptation.[6]

Again, it's about managing tradition *and* change:

> There is nothing inherently wrong with adhering to specific practices and strategies (indeed, we see tremendous consistency over time in great companies), but only if you comprehend the underlying why behind the practices, and thereby see when to keep them and when to change them.

An example of this in family businesses is the family constitution. When it is created, it is most important to develop a strong preamble that is easily understood and from which policies follow. Why? Because the preamble will help to identify under what circumstances policies might need to change for the benefit of the family *and* the business. So when it comes time to consider changes, there is an understanding of the intent of the constitution, the "why" in order to help know "what" portions of the constitution can be adjusted and under what conditions. In other words, not confusing the what and the why.

### *Seven Habits of Highly Effective People*

This book, by Stephen Covey, is aimed at solving personal and professional issues, and is based on a principle-centered approach comprising seven essential habits. In the late 1980s and 1990s this book became expected reading, and the basis of a course that nearly every up-and-coming business manager attended. One habit in particular speaks directly to the need to embrace conflicts, Habit 6: Synergize – principles of creative cooperation. Covey's definition of synergy is that:

> the whole is greater than the sum of its parts ... the relationship which the parts have to each other is a part in and of itself. It is not only a part, but the most catalytic, the most empowering, the most unifying and the most exciting.[7]

This concept is a key component in building the capacity and capability to manage paradoxes in an organization. The management of paradox, from Covey's point of view, is recognizing that managing both parts and seeing that as a part in and of itself, is where the power lies, what he calls "synergy."

Covey goes on to discuss compromise. Although compromise (detailed in the present book) is a way to approach a situation with opposing interests (like a paradox), it will yield less optimal results than would managing the interdependencies present. Covey draws an analogy that reinforces and illustrates this idea well:

> In interdependent situations compromise is the position usually taken. Compromise means that 1 + 1 = 1 1/2. Synergy means that 1+1 may equal 8, 16 or 1600.
>
> Seeking the third alternative is a major paradigm shift from the dichotomous, either/or mentality. But look at the difference in results. How much negative energy is typically expended when people try to solve problems or make decisions in an interdependent reality? ... It's like trying to drive down the road with one foot on the gas and the other foot on the brake! And instead of getting a foot off the brake, most people give it more gas. They try to apply more pressure, more eloquence, more logical information to strengthen their position. The problem is that highly dependent people are trying to succeed in an interdependent reality .... And synergy can't thrive in that environment .... The essence of synergy is to value the differences.

When dealing with paradoxes, interdependence of the opposing forces present is a given. From Covey's book, dealing with one of the two sides – the one that might seem to be more negative, given your current situation – can be a real obstacle to achieving goals. He refers to a scientific process to further explain.

> In an interdependent situation, synergy is particularly powerful in dealing with the negative forces that work against growth and change .... Sociologist Kurt Lewin developed a Force Field Analysis model in which he described any current level of performance as being a state of equilibrium between the driving forces that encourage upward movement and the restraining forces that discourage it. Driving forces generally are positive, reasonable, logical, conscious, and economic. In juxtaposition, restraining forces are often negative, emotional, illogical, unconscious, and social/psychological. Both sets of forces are very real and must be taken into account in dealing with change.
>
> Increasing the driving forces may bring results – for a while. But as long as the restraining forces are there, it becomes increasingly harder. It's like pushing against a spring: the harder you push, the harder it is to push until the force of the spring suddenly thrusts the level back down.

The force field analysis discussion in Covey's book is consistent with what happens in the case of ineffective paradox management: alternating from one solution to the other as the negatives associated with the choice made come to light. Covey emphasizes the need to recognize the interdependent opposites present in paradoxes and manage them to create synergy, which drives maximum business effectiveness: in other words, move to a Both/*AND* approach.

> But if you introduce synergy .... You can create an atmosphere in which to ... unfreeze them, loosen them up, and create new insights that actually transform those restraining forces into driving ones .... As a result, new goals, shared goals, are created, and the whole enterprise moves upward, often in ways that no one could have anticipated.
>
> Your own internal synergy is completely within the circle. You can respect both sides of your own nature – the analytical side and the creative side. You can value the differences between them and use that difference to catalyze creativity.

## *In Search of Excellence*

Authors Tom Peters and Robert Waterman studied many companies in the early 1980s to discern eight principles that the "best-run" companies employed. The *In Search of Excellence* principle about managing paradoxes is Principle 8: Simultaneous loose-tight properties:

> Any well-functioning organization is neither centralized nor decentralized but a wonderful combination of both. Around most dimensions the best companies, then and now, are loose. They give people exceptional freedom to do things their own way. At the same time, the great companies are highly centralized around a few crucial dimensions: the central values that make up their culture, one or two (no more) top strategic priorities, and a few key financial indicators.[8]

The authors go on to state:

> Simultaneous loose-tight properties, the last of our "eight basics" of excellent management practice, is mostly a summary point. It embraces much of what has come before and emerged, to our pleasant surprise, through the process of synthesis. It is in essence the co-existence of firm central direction and maximum individual autonomy – what we have called "having one's cake and eating it too." Organizations that live by the loose tight principle are on the one hand rigidly controlled, yet at the same time allow (indeed, insist on) autonomy, entrepreneurship, and innovation from the rank and file. They do this literally through "faith" – through value systems.
>
> They gave plenty of rope, but they accepted the chance that some of their minions would hang themselves. Loose–tight is about rope.

The "excellent" companies displayed a number of paradoxes, or as the book suggests, "These are the apparent contradictions that turn out in practice not to be contradictions at all." Several of the paradoxes discussed in *In Search of Excellence* are highlighted below:

- Autonomy *and* discipline:
  … autonomy is a product of discipline. The discipline (a few shared values) provides the framework. It gives people confidence (to experiment, for instance) stemming from stable expectations about what really counts.
  
  The "rules" in the excellent companies have a positive cast. They deal with quality, service, innovation and experimentation. Their focus is on building, expanding, the opposite of restraining; whereas most companies concentrate on controlling, limiting constraint. We

don't seem to understand that rules can reinforce positive traits as well as discourage negative ones, and that the former kind are far more effective.

- Small versus big (in other words, effectiveness versus efficiency): ... the efficiency/effectiveness contradiction dissolves in thin air. Things of quality are produced by craftsmen, generally requiring small-scale enterprise .... Activities that achieve cost efficiencies are reputedly best done in large facilities to achieve economies of scale ... small in almost every case is beautiful ... turns out to be the most efficient ... so we find in this most vital area, there really is no conflict.
- External versus internal:
  ... these companies are simultaneously externally focused and internally focused – externally in that they are truly driven by their desire to provide service, quality and innovative problem solving in support of their customers; internally in that quality control, is put on the back of the individual line worker ... service standards are likewise substantially self monitored. The organization thrives on internal competition ... intense communication, family feeling, open door policies, informality, fluidity and flexibility ... this constitutes the crucial internal focus ... on people.
- Security versus the need to stick out:
  By offering meaning as well as money, they give their employees a mission as well as a sense of feeling great. Every man becomes a pioneer, an experimenter, a leader. The institution provides guiding belief and creates a sense of excitement, a sense of being a part of the best, a sense of producing something of quality that is generally valued ... the average worker in these companies is expected to contribute, to add ideas, to innovate in service to the customer and in producing quality products ... each individual is expected to stand out and contribute, to be distinctive.

A key attribute of "excellent" companies, then, is their ability not only to manage the contradictions a paradox represents, but to harness them to drive high performance.

## IN SUMMARY

From Covey to Collins and Peters to Johnson, there is one thing in common, the need to manage paradoxes! The actual terms vary, but the meanings are the same. The implication is clear: we must view and manage paradoxical problems in the business environment differently. It is also clear that this does not mean that what has been used in the past should be thrown out, but rather that it must be broadened to include the identification, understanding, and management of paradoxes.

# Appendix C

# Family First–Business First Assessment

PROCESS

This Appendix presents a self-assessment (also discussed at the beginning of Part I) that can help family business members understand their current perspectives on the business *and* the family. Key details are presented below, including instructions for administration.

| | |
|---|---|
| What it is: | The assessment contains questions regarding orientation to family or to business in frequently controversial areas. |
| Who can use it: | Anyone associated with a family business: family members, owners, members of management, and others. |
| When it is helpful: | Can be helpful at a variety of points in the family business's evolution including:<br>❑ leadership transitions<br>❑ conflict resolution among members<br>❑ strategic crossroads. |
| Why use it: | The goal is to develop individual and collective understanding of the orientation to business and/or family, and how this might effect key decisions and processes. |

Follow these steps to administer the assessment.

Step 1 Distribute the survey, preferably in hard copy, to each respondent.

Step 2 Ask each respondent to read each question and circle a response reflecting their point of view.
(Note: If someone is unsure how to respond to a given question, have them use a rating of 3, the midpoint.)

Step 3 After respondents have completed both pages of the assessment, have them go back and total their ratings for the 14 business-first questions, and then for the 14 family-first questions.

Step 4 Use one of two possible follow-up approaches:

a. Open approach – Create a grid (like the one below) on a flip chart and have each respondent come forward as they are finished and record their score with a tally mark.

| Total for page | Business First | Family First |
|---|---|---|
| Total > 44 | | |
| 40–44 | | |
| Total < 40 | | |

b. Closed approach – Have everyone complete, total and pass their forms into the facilitator, who will then categorize final scores as above, but anonymously.

Step 5 After the responses are compiled and viewed by the broader group, you will have a set of data points around which to have a conversation. For example, you may find a split among the group: roughly half holding a business-first orientation for the business, and half holding a family-first orientation for the business. Talk about this by using examples. It may be revealed that those working in the business on a day-to-day basis have one view, while those not working in the business will have another, or one generation or branch will have one view, and others another, and so on.

Step 6 It's important to recognize that there's no right answer, there are only different points of view. Thus the first step in building better understanding among the family is gaining awareness of others' points of view. The next step is to understand the various factors that have brought about that particular point of view, from each side. Being aware of divergence (or convergence) in points of view – and the basis for each – can help the family plan for the business and itself.

**Table C.1** ***Family First–Business First Assessment, Part A: Business Issues for Family Businesses***

| | | | | | | | |
|---|---|---|---|---|---|---|---|
| 1 | Are you generous with shareholders in providing them with liquidity and dividends? | 1 | 2 | 3 | 4 | 5 | Or do you favor retention of capital in the business? |
| 2 | If a shareholder wants to redeem, does the share valuation formula provide a high price? | 1 | 2 | 3 | 4 | 5 | Or do you seek to keep shares at a low value? |
| 3 | Does your business focus on current profitability? | 1 | 2 | 3 | 4 | 5 | Or more on long-term growth? |
| 4 | Do you prefer a few diverse businesses? | 1 | 2 | 3 | 4 | 5 | Or one focused business? |
| 5 | Is your business mostly domestic? | 1 | 2 | 3 | 4 | 5 | Or are you more global? |
| 6 | Does your business prefer public privacy? | 1 | 2 | 3 | 4 | 5 | Or see visible public relations as important? |
| 7 | Do you prefer the decision-making speed of a private company? | 1 | 2 | 3 | 4 | 5 | Or the discipline and accountability of public ownership? |
| 8 | Do you do business with relatives who are suppliers or vendors or advisors? | 1 | 2 | 3 | 4 | 5 | Or prefer a strict no conflicts of interest policy? |
| 9 | Does your company regard loyalty highly? | 1 | 2 | 3 | 4 | 5 | Or, more so, celebrate achievement and merit? |
| 10 | Do you offer non-family executives a sense of career security? | 1 | 2 | 3 | 4 | 5 | Or reward them with stock options? |
| 11 | Are your decisions based heavily on family values? | 1 | 2 | 3 | 4 | 5 | Or, more so, on maximizing share price value? |
| 12 | Are you more respectful of tradition? | 1 | 2 | 3 | 4 | 5 | Or a promoter of change? |
| 13 | Is wealth preservation a key objective of owners? | 1 | 2 | 3 | 4 | 5 | Or is entrepreneurship more the focus? |
| 14 | Do you look for independent directors who are supportive in nature? | 1 | 2 | 3 | 4 | 5 | Or those who are more dispassionately critical of decisions and policies? |
| | Total score: | | | | | | |

***Source:*** Family First/Business First Assessment, John L. Ward, Family Business Consulting Group, 1999.

**Table C.1** ***Family First–Business First Assessment, Part B: Family Issues for Business-Owning Families***

| | | | | | | | |
|---|---|---|---|---|---|---|---|
| 1 | Do you welcome family employment regardless of work experience or educational qualifications? | 1 | 2 | 3 | 4 | 5 | Or have very selective family employment requirements before joining the business? |
| 2 | Is dissent accepted among family members so that different folks may express different views to management? | 1 | 2 | 3 | 4 | 5 | Or does the family attempt to be of one voice in communications to managers in the business? |
| 3 | Is ownership passed on by family branch (per stirpes)? | 1 | 2 | 3 | 4 | 5 | Or are there efforts that family members of future generations will have more equal ownership (per capita) regardless of size of different branches? |
| 4 | In decision making, is there respect for elders? | 1 | 2 | 3 | 4 | 5 | Or more aggressive "take charge" leadership? |
| 5 | Are non-employed owners involved in business decision making? | 1 | 2 | 3 | 4 | 5 | Or quite "hands off"? |
| 6 | Do family members feel that the business is part of their identity? | 1 | 2 | 3 | 4 | 5 | Or feel very autonomous from the business? |
| 7 | Does the family show a high standard of living? | 1 | 2 | 3 | 4 | 5 | Or deliberately attempt to understate its wealth? |
| 8 | Are policies and rules for family members flexible? | 1 | 2 | 3 | 4 | 5 | Or quite formal and precise? |
| 9 | Is compensation of family members private? | 1 | 2 | 3 | 4 | 5 | Or openly disclosed to family members and to managers? |
| 10 | Are there many unspoken topics and issues among family members? | 1 | 2 | 3 | 4 | 5 | Or open communications? |
| 11 | Is family attendance at family business events voluntary? | 1 | 2 | 3 | 4 | 5 | Or expected or required? |
| 12 | Does the extended family spend lots of time with each other away from the business? | 1 | 2 | 3 | 4 | 5 | Or do folks spend most all of their personal time with their nuclear family? |
| 13 | Do family members see the business as creating opportunities for personal freedom? | 1 | 2 | 3 | 4 | 5 | Or does it give them more a sense of personal responsibility? |
| 14 | Do family members use company resources for personal use? | 1 | 2 | 3 | 4 | 5 | Or is use of expense accounts, employees, or vehicles for personal use prohibited? |
| | Total score: | | | | | | |

***Source:*** Family First/Business First Assessment, John L. Ward, Family Business Consulting Group, 1999.

## SCORING

To interpret your scores, note that the questions on the first page are classic questions a business faces (Table C-1, Part A: Business Issues for Family Businesses). The higher your score, the more inclined you are to respond to these questions from a business-first point of view. The lower your score, the more you respond to these business issues from a family-first point of view. See Table C-2 to determine your focus.

**Table C.2** *Business First–Family First Assessment scoring*

| Page total | Your focus |
|---|---|
| Total > 44 | Business First |
| 40 – 44 | Not strongly Business or Family First |
| Total < 40 | Family First |

Similarly, the questions on the second page are questions faced by the family (Table C-1, Part B: Family Issues for Business-Owning Families). The higher your score, the more inclined you are to respond to these family issues from a business-first point of view. The lower your score, the greater your tendency to respond to these questions from a family-first point of view.

## TRENDS

From analyzing the results across countries, generations, and families over time, two themes have emerged.

- ❑ Family business members within a given culture share similar patterns of responses to the business first and family first questions.
- ❑ Despite this intra-cultural consistency in responses, there is also predictable variation among families surveyed within a culture.

Figure C-1 illustrates how national culture, the first bullet point, tends to shape responses to the assessment. There are five overall patterns

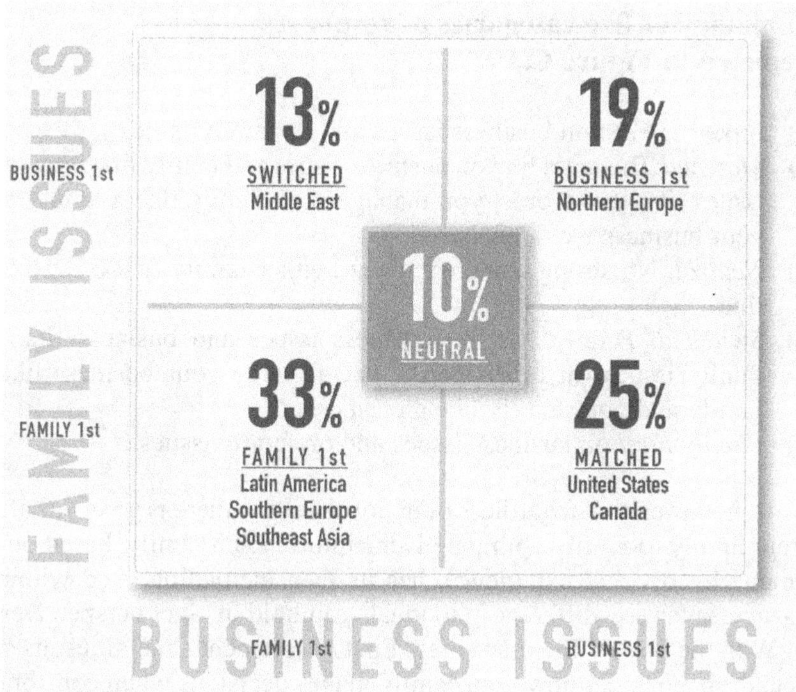


**Figure C-1** *Business First–Family First compiled assessment results*

of response summarized in Figure C-1. Please note that each of the five response patterns is represented in one of the five locations on the quadrant model. For example, Neutral, located in the middle of the quadrant model, represents no strong tendency toward either family first or business first.

## Summary of five categories of responses depicted in Figure C.1

- ❑ *Business First* on business issues and on family issues
- ❑ *Matched*: Business first on business issues and family first on family issues (in other words, you manage your family like a family and your business like a business)
- ❑ *Neutral*: No strong tendency toward either family first or business first
- ❑ *Switched*: Family first on business issues and business first on family issues (in other words, you manage your business like a family and your family like a business)
- ❑ *Family First* on business issues and on family issues.

Note, however, that regardless of national culture there is great variation from family to family within a given culture. Each family, based on its unique history and experience, has its own inclination. And within a particular family, different individuals can hold distinct perspectives.

With the Family First–Business First Assessment general results as a backdrop, consider how your family makes decisions when confronted with choices that impact both the family and the business. Does the option chosen (that is, business first or family first) depend on the type of problem faced? Or is the choice consistent no matter what the concern? At some point you may want to explore this issue further with family members. As mentioned earlier, Appendix C includes a clean copy of the Family First–Business First Assessment to use with your family group, along with a well-established process for conducting it.

As you face the special challenges of family business, it is valuable to know your own inclinations and those of the members, individually and collectively, of your family and executive team. Knowing your tendencies and those of others promotes careful attention to those who view issues differently. To be effective at managing paradoxes it is important to know your bias and to be able to empathize with others who see things from a different point of view. The self-assessment and other routes to awareness help uncover such biases.

# Appendix D
# More on Polarity Maps™

Over many years, Dr. Barry Johnson and Polarity Management Associates[1] have used Polarity Maps™ in a wide range of settings. Based on this experience, they have identified specific ways to apply the map to a variety of recurring dynamics. Here, several of the map-based approaches are reviewed and applied to classic family business conflicts and paradoxes.

## RESISTANCE TO CHANGE

Change isn't easy for most established systems, and family businesses are no exception. Even when a family recognizes the need to appreciate both sides of a paradox, there can be considerable resistance to embracing a historically non-preferred pole. The Polarity Map™ can be extremely useful in helping a family move beyond resistance to change, especially when they complete the map together.

Take the classic family business paradox of privacy *and* transparency. Many families in business have a strong preference for privacy, and are fiercely protective of information regarding the business and the family. They consider the confidentiality of business information a significant competitive advantage, and place a premium on personal privacy. Other family members, in contrast, may prefer transparency – they want to know what is going on in their business, in order to participate in decision making in a well-informed way. They may also want to share personal information openly, to promote more authentic and meaningful family relationships.

The paradox of privacy *and* transparency is a familiar point of potential family conflict. As discussed in Chapter 3, those working in the business frequently prefer privacy, and those not employed in the business tend to lean toward transparency. Early-stage businesses in Generations G1 and G2 are often focused on privacy. In later stages, a larger ownership group such as is often found in G3 often pushes for greater transparency. In many countries, the use of social networking tools by younger family members can feel threatening to older family members. In general, a push for change – especially toward more transparency – can evoke fear and strong resistance.

In this specific situation – and others involving resistance to change – the Polarity Map™ can be very useful in promoting a healthy Both/AND approach that transforms natural resistance into understanding and support for shared goals. To help address resistance in a family business situation, approach the map with the following steps (as illustrated in Figure D-1; quadrant labels match steps below):

A Start in the upside of the historically preferred pole (in this case, assume that it's privacy). Spend ample time exploring and appreciating the advantages of this side. Naturally, the group that has been resisting change will be most comfortable in this quadrant.

B Move diagonally, to the downside of the historically non-preferred pole (here, transparency). This should also be a comfortable quadrant for the resisting group.

C Next, move to the downside of the historically preferred pole (privacy). There will likely be some reluctance to describe the negatives of the historically preferred option, but the potential resistance should be diminished by steps A and B above.

D. Finally, the most difficult step: list the upsides of the historically non-preferred pole (transparency). There may still be resistance, and difficulty completing this quadrant, but the earlier steps should help the group through it.

This approach is very effective in reducing resistance to change, and potentially transforming it into support. The process of completing the map activates more of a Both/*AND* mindset. It helps a group accept the need for both the historically preferred side *and* its matched pair, the non-preferred side.

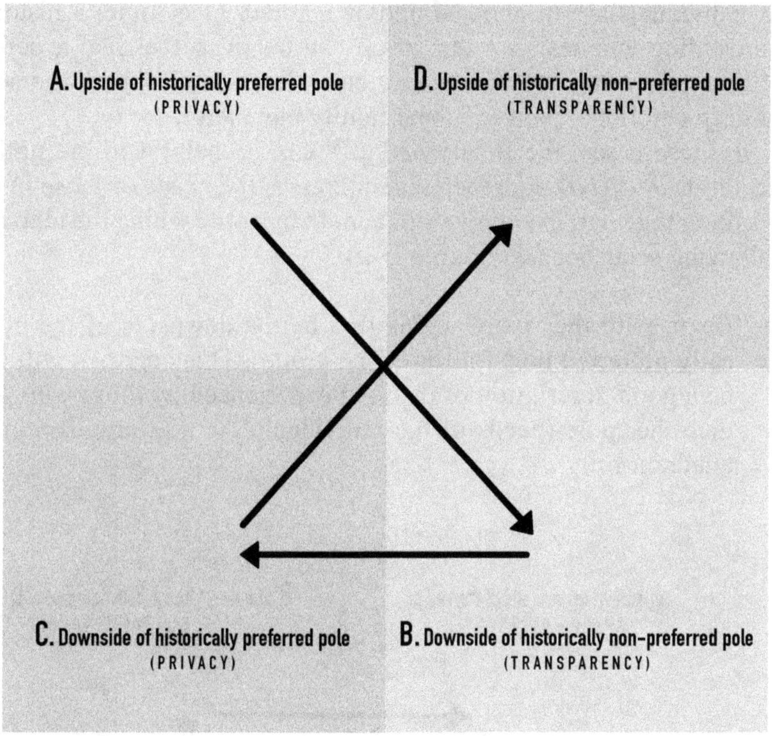


**Figure D-1** *Polarity Map™ sequence for handling resistance to change*

## PAINFUL SITUATIONS

It's hard to imagine a family that doesn't have to contend with a painful conflict at some point in their history. Many times, a paradox will be at the heart of the painful experience. Using the Polarity Map™ as a family group to gain a full appreciation of both sides of the paradox can be an extremely helpful process in such a situation.

The paradox of needs of the group *and* needs of the individual is a very common paradox for families in business together. Many families have a long history of emphasizing the needs of the group and ignoring the needs of individuals. In fact, some family businesses believe that they *must* emphasize the needs of the group in all circumstances, in order to survive. As a result, family members can feel that their needs as individuals are minimized and/or ignored. Over time, a historical, unrelenting emphasis on the group can begin to feel like a personal affront, an expression of a lack of care, "entrapment," and/or a source of deep emotional pain for some family members.

In these cases, the Polarity Map™ can be helpful in promoting a healthy Both/AND approach that addresses the needs of those in pain. Working together, the family will benefit by approaching the map in the following sequence (see Figure D-2):

A Begin with the "pain" – this will be the downside of the historically preferred pole (needs of the group). This quadrant will likely be a good description of the pain experienced by those who prefer the other pole (needs of the individual). As a group, explore this quadrant fully.

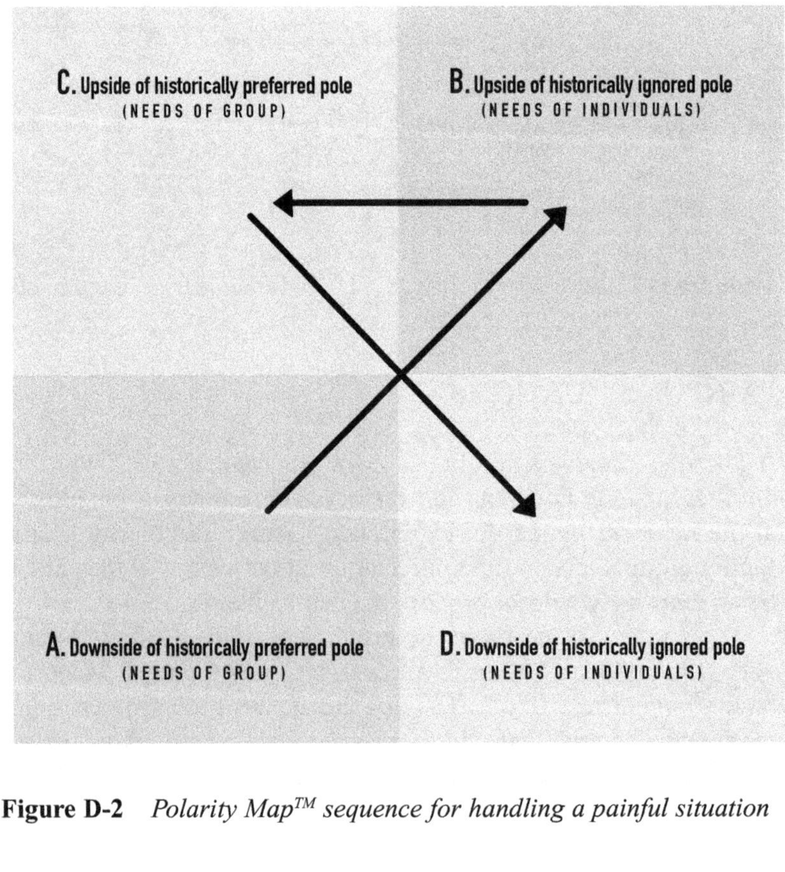


**Figure D-2** *Polarity Map™ sequence for handling a painful situation*

B Once individuals have had the chance to express their feelings, move to affirm the upsides of the historically ignored pole (needs of the individual). This may be the first time the group has acknowledged the upsides of this pole.

C Move to the upsides of the historically preferred pole (needs of the group) and explore it fully, to understand why many have favored this value in the past.

D End with the downsides of the historically ignored pole (needs of the individual).

This approach is effective in addressing situations involving pain and other negative emotions. The process of completing the map as a group activates more of a Both/*AND* mindset, and helps the group accept the need to honor both.

## BRINGING A GROUP TOGETHER

No matter how strong a family business may be, the many challenges faced over the years can pose a threat to the group's unity. The Polarity Map™ can be a useful tool for bringing the family team together, in the context of an overarching Both/AND mindset.

One common source of threat to family unity was explored in Chapter 3: the emergence, in the Cousin Collaboration Stage (G3), of a split between shareholders who are working in the business and those who are not. These two groups can develop very different priorities and perspectives, leading, in some cases, to group conflict.

One common area of tension in this context involves the paradox of harvest *and* invest. In some family businesses, a strong emphasis is placed upon investing over harvesting. Shareholders not working in the business are expected to be deferential to those working in the business, and expected to support an emphasis on investing. Historically, in these situations, shareholders with a preference for harvesting have had much less power and influence on the decision making in this area.

The Polarity Map™ can be very helpful in bringing groups together when they face an issue like this. The group should approach the map in the following sequence (see Figure D-3):

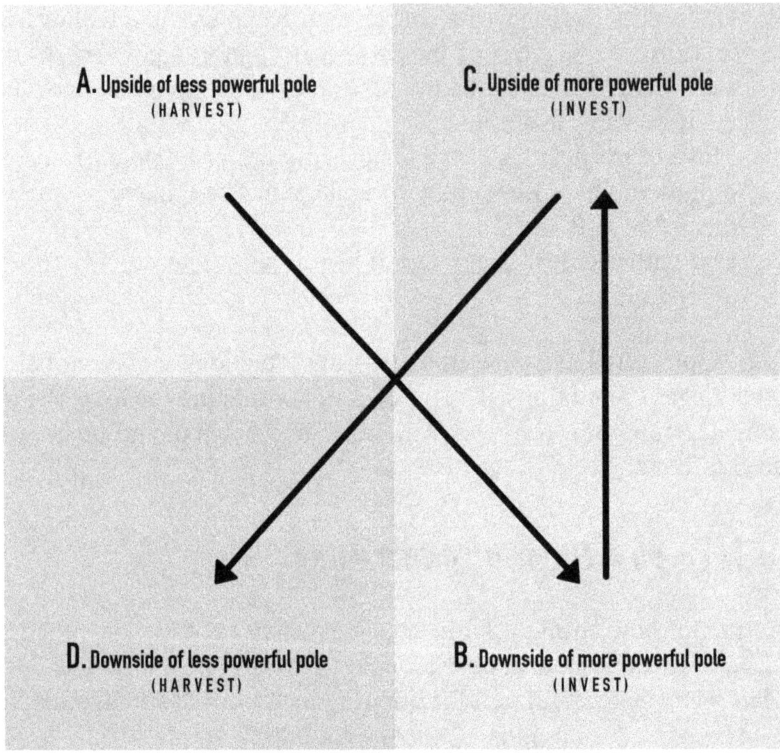


**Figure D-3** *Polarity Map™ sequence for bringing a group together*

A Start with the upside of the less powerful pole (harvest). Give these upsides a full hearing, with plenty of reinforcement.

B Move to the downside of the more powerful pole (invest). Again, this process will be one of strengthening and acknowledging those who often remain silent.

C Once the 'minority view' has been fully explored and appreciated in this way, move to the remaining upside of the more powerful pole (invest).

D Finally, complete the downside of the less powerful pole (harvest).

This sequence will allow the airing of perspectives that are often dismissed or never heard in the first place, whether consciously or unconsciously, by the group. The team is strengthened by genuinely welcoming every family member – and their perspectives.

## FUN USES OF THE MAP

### Walking the Map

There are many benefits to getting more *physical* in the experience of managing paradoxes using the Polarity Map™. For example, groups often have an "Aha" moment when they "walk the map." This begins with marking a Polarity Map™ on the floor, usually with masking tape, and designating the poles, along with their upsides and downsides. Start with the most comfortable quadrant, then walk the map together as a group, in the shape of the infinity sign, discussing each quadrant. This process is virtually guaranteed to provide valuable, unexpected insights.

### Using subgroups to complete a Map

To use the map in this way, gather participants in a room and create four subgroups. Assign each of the four quadrants to one of the subgroups, each representing one of the four quadrants. Have each group brainstorm the contents of their quadrant, then report to the broader team. As they report on their quadrant, the entire group should stand in the quadrant being described. One person can be designated to fill in the quadrants of the Polarity Map™ on a flipchart or computer as each group lists their content. This is a very quick, effective, involving way of completing a map and bringing a group together around the insights gained (Note: Figure D-4 contains a blank Polarity Map™ for future use).

Many thanks to Dr. Barry Johnson and Polarity Management Associates, who innovated these particular uses of the Polarity Map™.

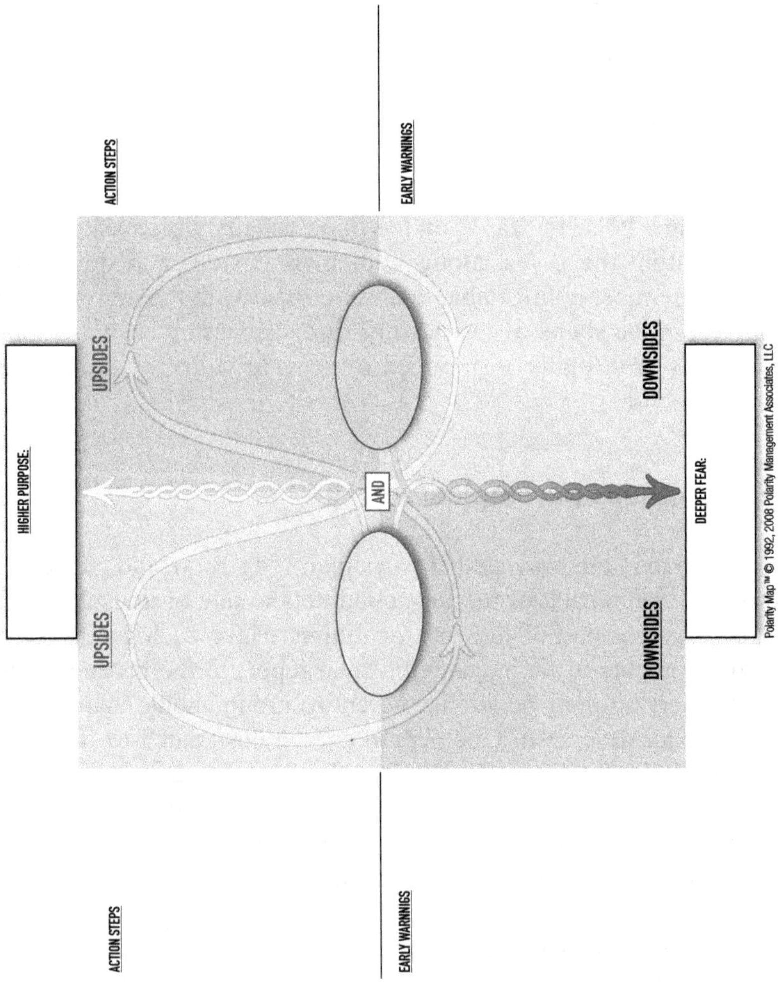


**Figure D-4** *Blank Polarity Map™*

# Notes

## Preface

1 Daniel H. Pink, *Drive* (New York: Riverhead Books, 2009), pp. 28–9.

## Introduction

1 Niels Bohr, The quotation is cited by L. I. Ponomarev, *The Quantum Dice* (London: IOP Publishing, 1993), p. 75.
2 John L. Ward, *Keeping the Family Business Healthy* (Georgia: Family Enterprise Publishers, 1997), pp. 1–3.
3 Richard Foster and Sarah Kaplan, *Creative Destruction* (New York: Doubleday, 2001), p. 8.
4 John L. Ward (ed.), *Unconventional Wisdom* (West Sussex: John Wiley, 2006), p. xix.
5 John L. Ward (ed.), *Unconventional Wisdom* (West Sussex: John Wiley, 2006), p. xix.
6 Dominic Dodd and Ken Favaro, *The Three Tensions* (USA: Jossey-Bass, 2007), p. 68.
7 Peter F. Drucker, *The Practice of Management* (New York: Harper & Row, 1954), p. 342.
8 Barry Johnson, *Polarity Management: Identifying and Managing Unsolvable Problems* (Amherst, Mass.: HRD Press, 1996), and Polarity Management Associates, www.polaritymanagement.com.
9 Greg Page, 'The business of paradox', *Cargill News,* vol. 70, no. 4 (Jan–Feb 2006), p. 4.
10 Eric Fromm, *Man for Himself: An Inquiry Into the Psychology of Ethics* (USA: First Owl, 1990), p. 45.
11 Pierre Wack, "Scenarios: uncharted waters ahead," *Harvard Business Review* (September–October 1985), p. 72.
12 Greg Page, 'The business of paradox', *Cargill News*, vol. 70, no. 4 (Jan–Feb 2006), p. 5.
13 Robert L. Heilbroner, *The Worldly Philosophers*, 6th edn (New York: Touchstone, 1991), p. 142.
14 Hirotaka Takeuchi, Emi Osono, and Norihiko Shimizu, "The contradictions that drive Toyota's success," *Harvard Business Review* (June 2008), p. 98. (Information and charts derived from this article.)
15 In early 2010, Toyota faced several high-profile product-line challenges including large-scale recalls. Around this time, Akio Toyoda, great-grandson of the company's founder, became Toyota's new president, the first Toyoda family president in over a decade. Toyoda immediately noted how the company might have "stretched" too far in seeking to unseat GM as the world's number one

carmaker, likely contributing to recent quality issues. As president Toyoda works to renew his company's emphasis on quality and customer satisfaction, he will likely have to reinforce an environment that embraces contradictions – such as that between tradition and change, a major focus of this book (John L. Ward, "Putting family back into Toyota strategy," *Family Business Advisor,* vol. 18, issue 9 (September 2009), p. 7).

## Part I

1 Charles Handy, *The Age of Paradox* (Boston, Mass.: Harvard Business School Press, 1994), pp. 11–12.

## Chapter 1

1 Richard Farson, *Management of the Absurd* (New York: Touchstone, 1997), pp. 23–4.
2 John L. Ward and Colleen Lief, *IMD–3–1495 Prudence and audacity: The house of Beretta*, International Institute for Management Development, v. 21.02.2005, 2005. (All graphics and detail regarding Beretta were taken from this case.)

## Chapter 2

1 Axel Johnson, *AB Annual Report*, 2009, back cover.
2 Adi Godrej, 'India: Change is constant', *Campden FB*, no. 42 (April 2009), p. 27.
3 John L. Ward (ed.), *Unconventional Wisdom* (West Sussex: John Wiley, 2006).
4 T. K. Das, *The Subjective Side of Strategy Making: Future Orientations and Perceptions of Executives* (New York: Praeger, 1986).
5 A. Gonzalez and P. G. Zimbardo, "Time in perspective: A *Psychology Today* survey report," *Psychology Today*, 19, (1985), pp. 21–6.
6 Quoted from Bernard S. Raskas (ed.), *Living Thoughts: Inspiration, Insight, and Wisdom from Sources Throughout ...* (University of California: Hartmore House, 1976), p. 111.

## Part II

1 John L. Ward, *Perpetuating The Family Business: 50 Lessons Learned from Long Lasting, Successful Families in Business* (Basingstoke: Palgrave Macmillan, 2004), pp. 8–9.

## Chapter 3

1 Adam Bellow, *In Praise of Nepotism: A Natural History* (USA: Doubleday, 2003), p. 467.
2 David McCullough, *John Adams* (New York: Simon & Schuster, 2001), pp. 236–7.
3 Crawford Hill, "Bancroft cousin's letter: paying the price for our passivity," *Wall Street Journal,* online edition, July 27, 2007.
4 John L. Ward, "The ultimate vision for continuity?" *Families in Business*, Sep./Oct. 2003, pp. 78–9.

## Chapter 4

1 Mary Parker Follett, *Dynamic Administration: The Collected Papers of Mary Parker Follett,* ed. Elliot M. Fox and L. Urwick (London: Pitman, 1973), pp. 30–1.
2 J. Davis and R. Tagiuri, "The influence of life stages on father–son work relationships in family companies" (unpublished manuscript, Graduate School of Business Administration, University of Southern California, 1982).
3 Bank of Korea study (reference: Han-Kook News Paper), copyright 2009 Japan-i.jp.

## Part III

1 Saint Teresa of Avila (born March 28, 1515) was a prominent Spanish mystic, Carmelite nun, and writer of the Counter Reformation. She was a reformer of the Carmelite Order and is considered, along with John of the Cross, a founder of the Discalced Carmelites. In 1970 she was named Doctor of the Church.

## Chapter 5

1 Oliver Wendell Holmes, unsourced.
2 James O'Toole, *The Exectutives's Compass: Business and the Good Society* (New York: Oxford University Press, 1995), p 5.

## Chapter 6

1 Dr. Barry Johnson, "Polarity management: one tool for managing complexity and ambiguity," Polarity Management Associates, 2001, p. 8.
2 Main sources for this chapter: Barry Johnson, *Polarity Management: Identifying and Managing Unsolvable Problems* (Amherst, Mass.: Human Resource Development Press, 1996); Roy. M. Oswald and Barry Johnson, *Managing Polarities in Congregations: Eight Keys for Thriving Faith Communities* (Herndon, Va.: Alban Institute, 2010); and Polarity Management Associates, www.polarity management.com.

## Part IV

1 PriceWaterhouse Change Integration Team, *The Paradox Principles* (Chicago, Ill.: Irwin, 1996), pp. 18–19.

## Chapter 7

1 Robert Bolton, unsourced.

## Appendix A

1 Benjamin Schuman-Stoler researched much of the material for and wrote this Appendix. The authors thank him for his support.
2 Alexandre Kojeve, *Introduction to the Reading of Hegel: Lectures on the Phenomenology of Spirit,* trans. James H. Nichols, Jr., (Ithaca, N.Y.: Cornell University Press, 1980), pp. vii–74.
3 Immanuel Kant, "Critique of aesthetical judgment," in *Philosophies of Art and*

*Beauty: Selected Readings in Aesthetics from Plato to Heidegger*, ed. Albert Hofstadter and Richard Kuhns (Chicago, Ill.: University of Chicago Press, 1964), pp. 279–96.

4 Immanuel Kant, *To Perpetual Peace: A Philosophical Sketch,* trans. Ted Humphrey (Indianapolis: Hackett, 2003), pp. vii–37.

5 Glen Jeansonne, *A Time of Paradox; America Since 1890* (Lanham, Md.: Rowman & Littlefield, 2006), pp. xix–xxxiii, 515–20.

6 Sandro Petruccioli, *Atoms, Metaphors, and Paradoxes; Niels Bohr and the Construction of a New Physics* (Cambridge: Cambridge University Press, 1993), pp. 1–35.

7 Frederick Turner, *Shakespeare's Twenty–first Century Economics – The Morality of Love and Money* (New York: Oxford University Press, 1999).

8 All quotes from the Dalai Lama, *The Power of Compassion; A Collection of Lectures by His Holiness the XIV Dalai Lama*, trans. Geshe Thupten Jinpa (New Delhi, India: HarperCollins India, 1995), pp. 1–118.

9 Mantak Chia and Tao Huang, *The Secret Teachings of the Tao Te Ching* (Rochester, Vt: Destiny, 2005), pp. 1–25, 201–35.

## Appendix B

1 Jag Sheth, Raj Sisodia, and David B. Wolfe, *Firms of Endearment* (New Jersey: Wharton School Publishing, 2007), pp. 236, 242, 243, 245, and 250.

2 Bala Chakravarthy and Peter Lorange, *Profit or Growth?* (New Jersey: Wharton School Publishing, 2008), pp. 13, 161, 162, 164.

3 Dominic Dodd and Ken Favaro, *The Three Tensions* (USA: Jossey-Bass, 2007), pp. xii, xv, 199.

4 Jim Collins, *Good to Great* (New York: HarperCollins, 2001), pp. 20, 22, 13, 142, 152.

5 Jim Collins and Jerry I. Porras, *Built to Last* (New York: HarperCollins, 1994), pp. XIV, XV, 1, 2, 44, 45, 85, 86.

6 Jim Collins, *How the Mighty Fall* (New York: HarperCollins, 2009), p. 36.

7 Stephen Covey, *The Seven Habits of Highly Effective People* (New York: Simon & Schuster, 1989), pp.. 263, 271, 274, 279–80, 283.

8 Thomas J. Peters and Robert H. Waterman, Jr., *In Search of Excellence* (New York: HarperCollins, 2004/1982), p. 4 Authors' Note: Excellence 2003, 318, 319, 321, 322, and 323.

## Appendix C

1 Family First/Business First Assessment, John L. Ward, Family Business Consulting Group, 1999.

## Appendix D

1 Sources: Barry Johnson, *Polarity Management: Identifying and Managing Unsolvable Problems* (Amherst, Mass: Human Resource Development Press, 1992); Roy. M. Oswald and Barry Johnson, *Managing Polarities in Congregations: Eight Keys for Thriving Faith Communities* (Herndon, Va.: Alban Institute, 2010); and Polarity Management Associates, www.polarity management.com.

# Index


A
acceptance, conflicts over, 26
accountability, culture of, 122
action *and* planning paradox, 58
Action Steps, 123–5, 132
Adams, John, 53
algorithmic problem solving, xii, 8–9, 97–8, 140
Amazon, 169
ambiguity, attitudes to, 3, 7–8, 10
art, judgment of, 157
auto parts example, 116–28
autonomy *and* discipline paradox, 182
Axel Johnson, Inc., 36

B
Balance approach, 103, 108, 110, 112
Bancroft family, 53
Bank of Korea, 79–80
banking example, 24
Bellow, Adam, 53
benchmarking, 112
Beretta, 32–4, 42–3, 44, 46–8, 149
board of directors, 84–5, 91
Bohr, Niels, 1, 160
Bolton, Robert, 139
both, concept of, xi, 23–5, 31, 48, 64, 73
  Both/*And* approach, 78, 98, 99–101, 103–6, 113, 119, 169, 177, 193
brain, human, 164
brainstorming, 198
Buddhism, 163–4
*Built to Last*, 168, 176–9
business(es)
  adapted to suit family needs, 24, 29
  business-first focus, 22–3, 53, 60–1, 74–5, 108, 110, 112, 122, 128
  literature, paradoxes in, 167–84
  norms, beliefs *and* values of, 21
  *see also* family business

C
candor *and* diplomacy paradox, 151
capital, business need for, 1
  *see also* harvest *and* invest paradox
career
  coach, 105, 106
  outside the family business, 23, 105
  planning, 31, 82, 125, 130
  within the family business, 23
  *see also* employment
Cargill, 5–7, 9–10, 149, 176
  Cargill News,6–7, 9–10
Chakravarthy, Bala, 168, 170–2
change
  as evolution *and* innovation, 46–7
  Hegel's view of, 10
  and succession in leadership, 40
  *and* tradition *see* tradition *and* change
Chia, Mantak, 165
Choice approach, 102, 108, 110, 112
Collins, Jim, 168, 172, 174–9
communication
  culture of, 68, 148–9
  difficulties in, 57, 69–70
  importance of, 165
  skills, 147
  *see also* privacy *and* transparency paradox
compensation
  of family members, 70, 81–2
  high levels of, 169–70
Compromise approach, 102–3, 108, 110, 112, 180
conflict (in family businesses), xiii–xiv, 26–8
  examples of, 28
  in families, 22, 116
  fundamental between family and business, 26–7

in the intersections, 76–91, 150
intolerance of, 116
management skills, 147
Polarity Map for handling, 193–6
productive, 76
construction business example, 141–2
control *and* trust paradox, 57, 87
Copenhagen approach, 160–1
core *and* opportunistic paradox, 64
corporate cycle, 173
corporate governance
process creation, 83
structure example, 37
*see also* governance
cost versus quality paradox, 7
Costco, 169
cousin collaborations, 54
Cousin Collaboration Stage, 55, 67–72, 196
Covey, Stephen R., 168, 179–81
creativity, 1
systematic, 33
culture
of Beretta, 46–8
famiy business, xii–xiii, 141–9
impact of, 140–9, 189–91
judgmental versus curious, 144
national, 189–90
curiosity, 143–4
customer benefit, 173

**D**

Dalai Lama, 163–4
Davis, J., 77
Deeper Fear statements, 125–6, 133
Descartes, Rene, 161
diagonal assets, 173
dialectical process, 10–11, 155–6
dividend/distribution, 69, 84–5, 91, 109–10
*see also* harvest *and* invest paradox
Dodd, Dominic, 5, 168, 173–4
Dow Jones & Company, 53
Drucker, Peter, 5, 76

**E**

Early Warnings, 123–5, 132
Edinburgh, Prince Philip, duke of, 42
education
budget, 146
of family members, 129, 146
requirements, 101–2
*see also* training
effectiveness versus efficiency paradox, 183
Einstein, Albert, 160
either/or, *see under* problem solving
employment
of family members, 28–9, 81–2, 89, 91, 100–7
hiring strategies, 141–2
Enterprising Family, 25, 72–4, 89, 149, 151, 178
equality *and* merit paradox, 27, 67, 86, 87
estate planning, 66, 89
evolution *and* innovation paradox, 46
external *and* internal paradox, 183

**F**

family
aid to members in need, 89
alienated from business, 22
or business first, 21–35
*and* business intersection, 26–7
constitution/charter, 89, 179
culture, xii–xiii, 141–9
first focus, 23, 74–5, 108, 110, 112
intranet, 146
*and* management conflicts, 80–3, 91
member employment *see under* employment
member roles, varied, 25, 104
norms, beliefs *and* values of, 21
one family vs branches paradox, 71
*and* ownership conflicts, 85–8, 91
unity, reinforcing, 87, 196–7
values *and* vision, 89
family business
competitive advantage of, 32
continuity orientation, 79–80, 139–40

culture, 141–9
as oxymoron, 2
typical features of, 2, 38
typical successes of, 2
values, examples of, 45
family council, 104, 106
composition, 130–1
family meetings, 86–7, 91, 111–12, 116, 147
examples of, 68–9, 116
Family First–Business First Assessment, 17–19, 34–5, 102, 185–91
Farson, Richard, 21
Favaro, Ken, 5, 168, 173–4
*Firms of Endearment*, 168–70
Fitzgerald, F. Scott, 6
fixed *and* flexible paradox, 87
Fletcher, Jerry, 168
Follett, Mary Parker, 76–7
force field analysis, 181
formal *and* informal paradox, 70
Founding Stage businesses, 55–61
freedom *and* loyalty paradox, 71
French Revolution, 156
Fromm, Erich, 7
Fusion approach, 106–8, 110, 112, 129–30, 150–1

G

generational transition, 27–8, 53–75, 149
generational characteristics, 53
generational oscillation, 54–6, 73, 150
genogram, 67
globalization, impact of, xi
Godrej Group, 37–8
Gonzalez, A., 39
*Good to Great*, 168, 174–6
governance issues, 83, 85
structures, 88–90
*see also* corporate governance
growth strategies, 169–70
growth versus liquidity/profitability paradox, 1, 5, 170–2, 173–4

**H**

Handy, Charles, 17, 21
harvest *and* invest paradox, 69, 71, 84, 109, 196–7
*Harvard Business Review*, 8–9, 11
Hegel, G. W. H., 10, 155–6
heuristic problem solving, xii, 9, 98, 113, 140
*see also* both
Hewlett-Packard, 176
Higher Purpose statements, 125–6, 133
Hill, Crawford, 53
hiring strategies, 141
Holmes, Oliver Wendell, 97
*How the Mighty Fall,* 168, 179
Huang, Tao, 165

**I**

*in-laws, 82, 87, 117*
*In Search of Excellence*, 168, 181–3
inclusion *and* exclusion paradox, 87
inclusive *and* selective paradox, 104
individual *and* collective paradox, 30–2, 67, 151, 193–6
information sharing between family members, 69
*see also* communication
infinity loop, 121–3, 132
Integration approach, 104–5, 107–8, 110, 112, 128, 143, 151
international relations, realism *and* idealism in, 158–9
internship, 106, 117–28

**J**

Japanese family firms, 79–80
Jeansonne, Glen, 159–60
Jet Blue, 169
Johnson, Barry, 5, 115, 117, 168, 192, 198
Johnson & Johnson, 168, 176

**K**

Kant, Immanuel, 157–8, 161
Kennan, George F., 159
Kleisterlee, Gerard, 171–2

**L**

LaoTzu, 164–5

leaders, training of future, 32, 42
leadership
Level 5, 174–5
qualities of, 8, 9
succession, 27–8, 40–2, 62, 68
Level 5 leadership, 174–5
Levi Strauss, 176
Lewin, Kurt, 181
Lief, Colleen, 46
Limbardo, P. G., 39
Lincoln, Abraham, 175
Locke, John, 161
loose–tight properties, 181–2
Lorange, Peter, 168, 170–2

**M**
Machiavelli, Noccolo, 159
management
as a business subsystem, 76
*and* family conflicts, 80–3, 91
*and* ownership conflicts, 83–5, 91
paradox management, 167–8
philosophies of, 43
styles, 5, 62–3
market *and* need paradox, 82
Marx, Karl, 155
Medtronic, 172
merit *and* equality paradox, 65, 85
metalworking industry example, 31–2
moral issues, 157–8
basic human good qualities, 163–4
Mosby, David, 168
Murdoch, Rupert, 53

**N**
Napoleon Bonaparte, 156
neuroscience, 161
News Corporation, 53

**O**
O'Neil, John R., 168
O'Toole, James, 97
Olwyler, Kelle, 168
ownership
agreements, 89
conflicts over, 28, 83–8, 91
and decision-making model, 70
economic and emotional, 85–6
rights to, 86

**P**
Page, Greg, 5–7, 10
paradox
across the generations, 53–75
action *and* planning, 58
ambiguity *and* uncertainty in, 3, 7–8
in Buddhism, 163–4
in business literature, 167–84
choice of both sides, xi
classic paradoxes for family businesses, xii, 2–3, 29, 74, 150
continuum for addressing, 97–114
and contradictions in intersections, 77–9
definition, xii, 4
and energy in tension, 10
in family life, 4–5
historical perspective on, 10, 12, 155–66
key impact areas, 75
management continuum, 101
management cycle of renewal, 113
and points of conflict, xiii
scientific, 160–1
in Shakespeare, 161–3
Stockdale, 175
underlying other paradoxes, 171
versus solvable problem, 5–6, 7
*see also* individual paradoxes: autonomy *and* discipline, candor *and* diplomacy, control *and* trust, core *and* opportunistic, cost versus quality, effectiveness versus efficiency, equality *and* merit, evolution *and* innovation, external *and* internal, fixed *and* flexible, formal *and* informal, freedom *and* loyalty, growth versus liquidity/profitability, harvest *and* invest, inclusion *and* exclusion, inclusive *and*

selective, individual *and* collective, loose–tight properties, market *and* need, merit *and* equality, one family vs branches, privacy *and* transparency, proprietorship *and* stewardship, representation *and* qualifications, roots *and* wings, selective *and* inclusive, self-confidence *and* egotism, tradition *and* change, universal *and* relative, whole *and* parts, work *and* fun
pay *see* compensation
Peters, Thomas J., 168, 181–3
Petrucciolo, Sandro, 160
philanthropy, 25
plan, do, check, act, 97
plastics manufacturing example, 43–4
Plato, 6
Polarity Management Associates, 115, 192, 198
Polarity Map, 100, 104, 115–34, 150, 193–200
  blank, 199
  step-by-step guidelines, 132–3
  "walking," 198
Porras, Jerry I., 168, 172, 176–9
PriceWaterhouse, 137
pricing, 41
privacy *and* transparency paradox, 69–70, 192–3
problem
  conflict, contradiction, paradox, 78
  different ways of treating, 3
  lifecycle of, 8
  not meant to be solved, 9
  solvable versus paradox, 5, 7
problem solving, xi, 97–8, 174
  culture of, 146
  difficulty with paradoxes, xiii
  either–or approaches, 99–101, 108
  two types of skills, xii
  ways of treating different problems, 3, 8–9, 21–2
  *see also* algorithmic problem solving, both
*Profit or Growth*, 168, 170–2
proprietorship *and* stewardship paradox, 58

**R**

representation *and* qualifications paradox, 84
responsibility, personal, 47–8
roots *and* wings paradox, 4, 59, 81–2
Royal Dutch Shell, 9–10
Royal Phillips Electronics, 171

**S**

sale of businesses, 22, 53
selective *and* inclusive paradox, 81, 82, 108
self-assessment inventory, 17–20, 34–5, 185–91
self-confidence *and* egotism paradox, 164
*Seven Habits of Highly Effective People*, 168, 179–81
Shakespeare, William, 161–3
Sheth, Jag, 168–70
Sibling Partnership Stage, 55, 61–7
Sisodia, Raj, 168–70
skills to manage paradoxes, 3
social networking, 193
socialistic *and* capitalistic approaches, conflict between, 26–7, 76
Socrates, 156
spiritual life, 95
stakeholders, 127, 170
  family's evolution as, 77
Stockdale paradox, 175
strategy
  business oriented by family concerns, 24
  formulation process, 42–3
  internally drive, 47
  strategic planning approach, 24, 64
  traditional business vs family business, 43
Strauss, 45
structure of the book, 13
succession *see* generational transition, leadership succession

Sun Tzu, 158
sustainable earnings, 173
synergy, 180–1
Synthesis approach, 105–6, 107–8, 110, 112, 129, 143, 151, 182

**T**
Taiguri, R., 77
Taoism, 164–5
taxation issues, 82
technology accelerators, 176
Teresa of Avila, Saint, 95
three–circle model, 77–8
*Three Tensions, The*, 168, 173–4
Timberl*and*, 168
time horizon
  *and* Eastern thought, 163
  of family businesses, 2, 38–40, 145, 147, 173
  integration of contradictions over long, 11
  of problem-solving approaches, 98–100
Toyota, 11–12, 145, 168
Trader Joe's, 169
tradition *and* change paradox, 4, 13, 36–48, 151, 175, 178–9
  statements of, 42
training
  at company universities, 178
  for family members, 32, 68, 101–6
  *see also* internship
transportation company example, 56–74
trust, culture of, 63–4, 147–8
trusts, use of, 87

**U**
United States, as the ultimate paradox, 159–60
universal *and* relative paradox, 164

V
values
  Beretta's, 46–7
  in family *and* other businesses, 44–5
  review of, 144
  statements, 89
virtuous *and* vicious cycles, 126, 130, 133
visionary companies, 176–7
Voltaire, 156

**W**
*Wall Street Journal,* 53
Walmart, 176
Ward, John, 46, 51
Waterman, Robert H., 168, 181–3
Wegman, 170
Weissman, Michael, 168
whole *and* parts paradox, 173
Wilson, Woodrow, 159
Wolfe, David B., 168–70
work *and* fun paradox, 86–7, 112
work–life balance, 59, 65

**Z**
Zimbardo, Philip, 168